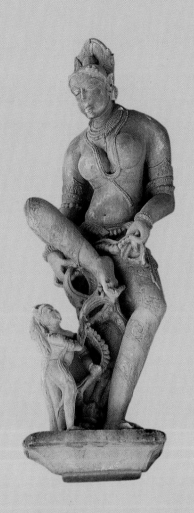

Khajuraho

The Art of Love

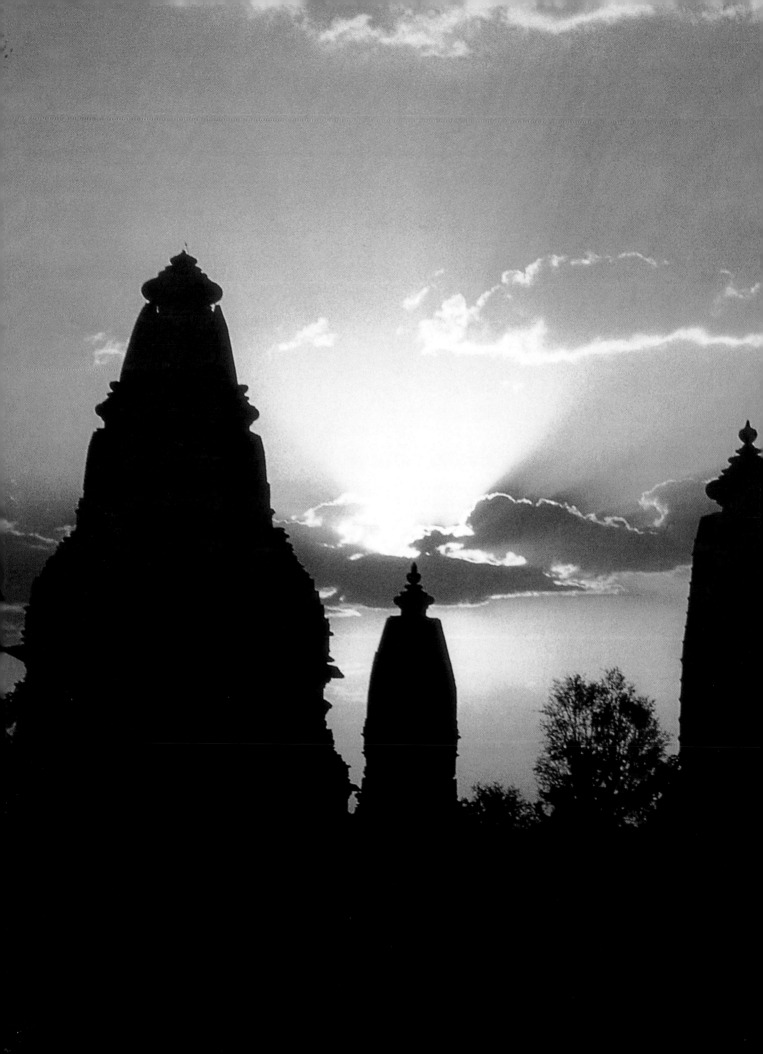

Khajuraho

The Art of Love

Prakash Books

Published by Prakash Book Depot
M-86, Connaught Circus
New Delhi-110001
Ph: (011) 3326897, Fax: (011) 3326566
E-mail: pbdepot@giasdl01.vsnl.net.in

Designed by: Yogesh Gajwani and Suraksha Gajwani

ISBN 81-7234-022-2

Printed at Thomson Press (I) Ltd.

PHOTO CREDITS

Surender Sahai : All pictures except those mentioned below.

Thomas Dix : 1, 6-7, 8-9, 10-11, 18-Above, 23-Below, 27-Left, 28-29, 34-Above
(also on page 38), 38-Below, 42-Right, 46, 49-Above Right, 65, 68-69, 70-Above,
71-Left, 71-Right, 72-Left Above, 72-Left Below, 73-Below (also on page 28-29),
74, 76-77, 79, 80-Above, 82-Below, 84-85, 86-87, 89, 90, 94-Right

Subhash Bhargava : 16, 17, 18-Below, 22, 27-Right, 32, 34-Left, 35-Right, 36-37,
39, 41, 44-45, 50-Above, 50-Below, 51, 52-53, 55, 57, 58, 66, 67, 95

Pankaj Shah : 2-3, 4-5, 12-13, 19, 20-21, 24, 31, 33, 43, 47, 48, 59, 63, 64,
70-Below, 72-Right, 73, 75-Above, 75-Below, 80-Below, 81, 82-Above (also on
page 19), 83, 88-Above, 91-Left Below, 91-Right Below, 92-93, 94-Above, 96

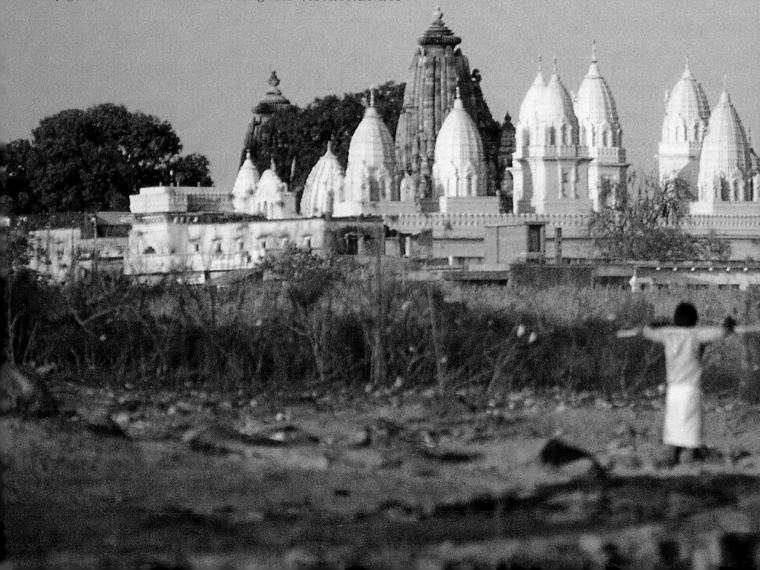

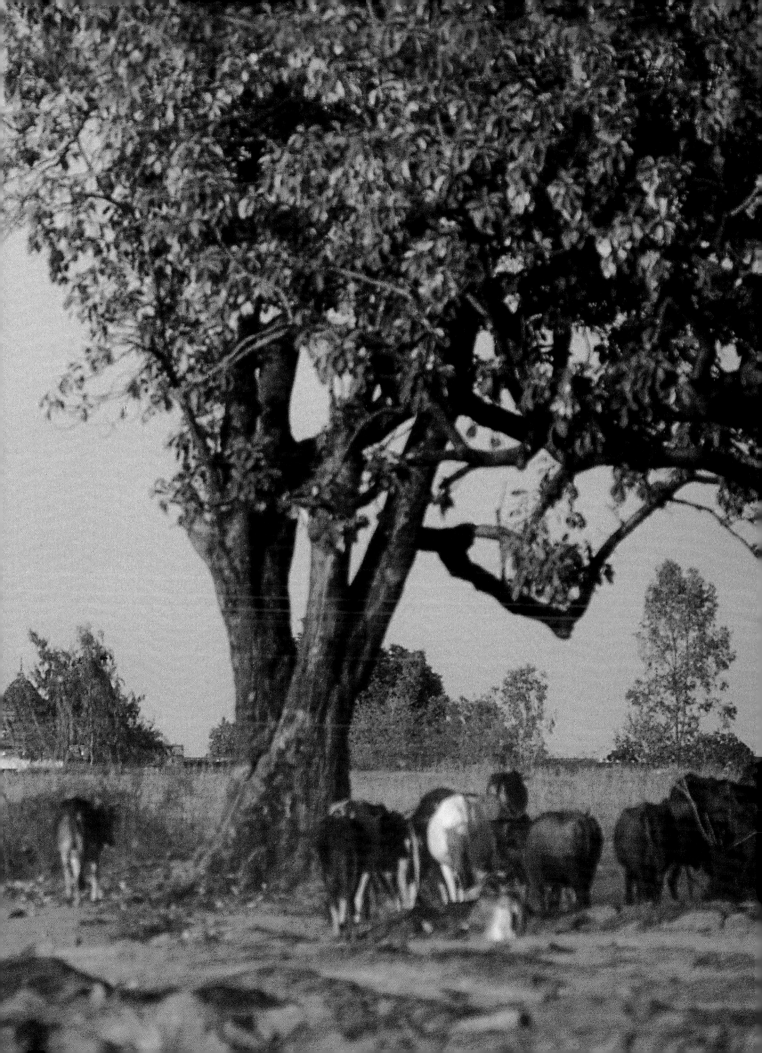

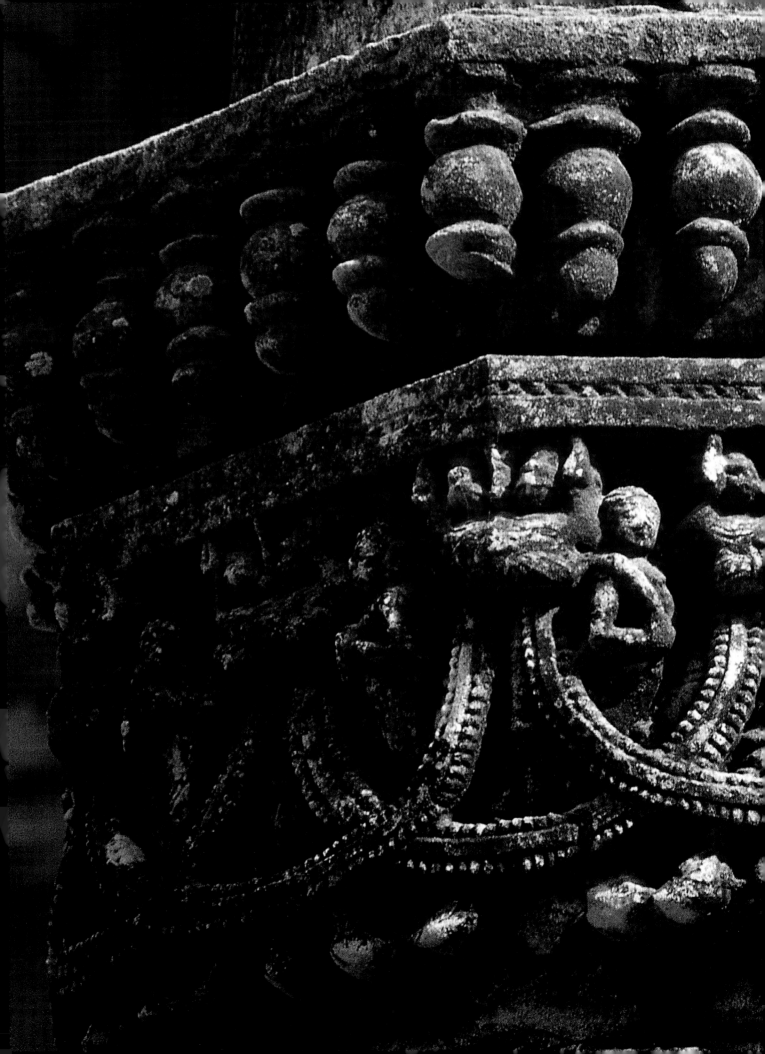

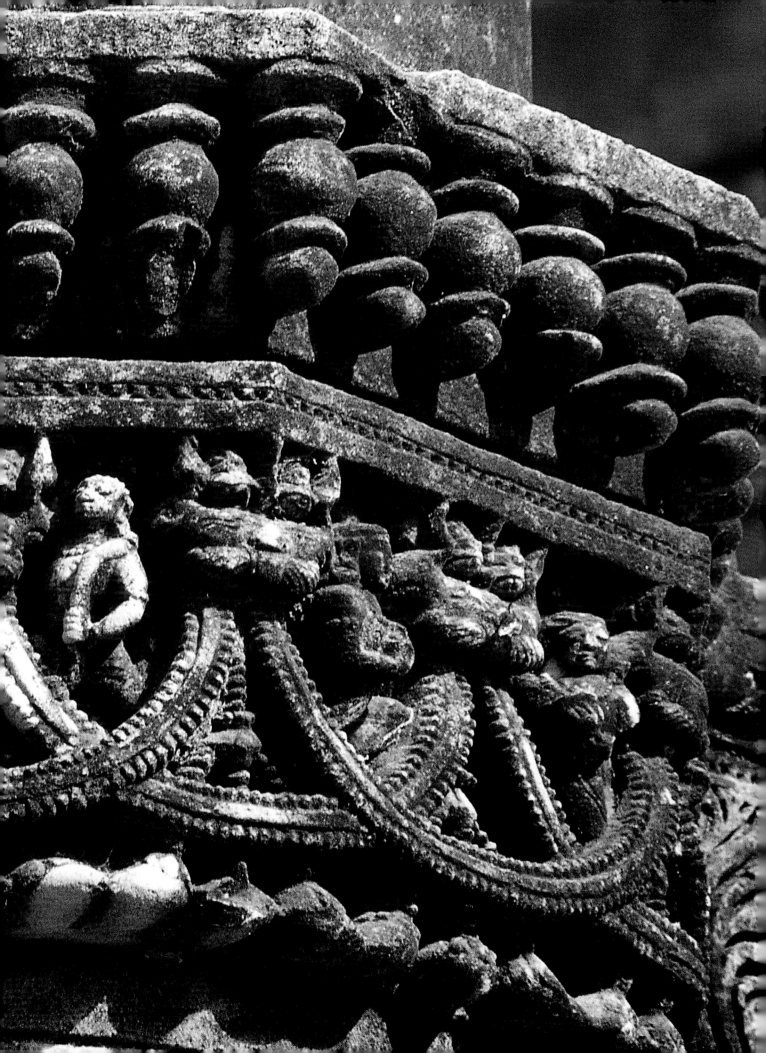

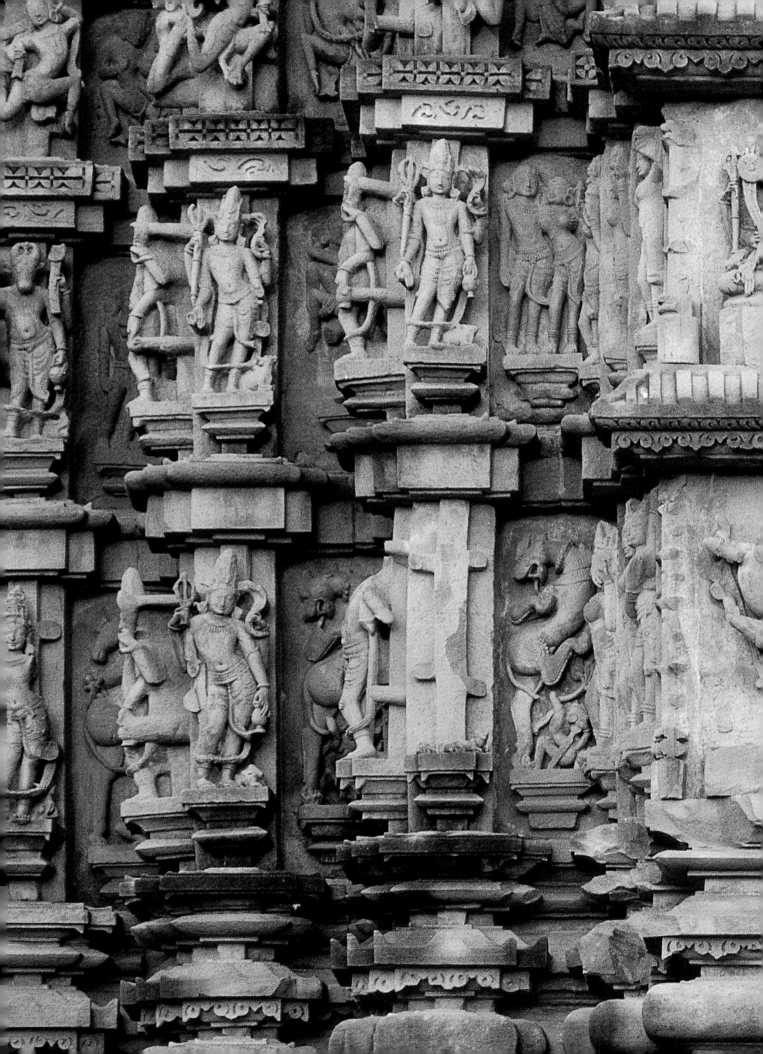

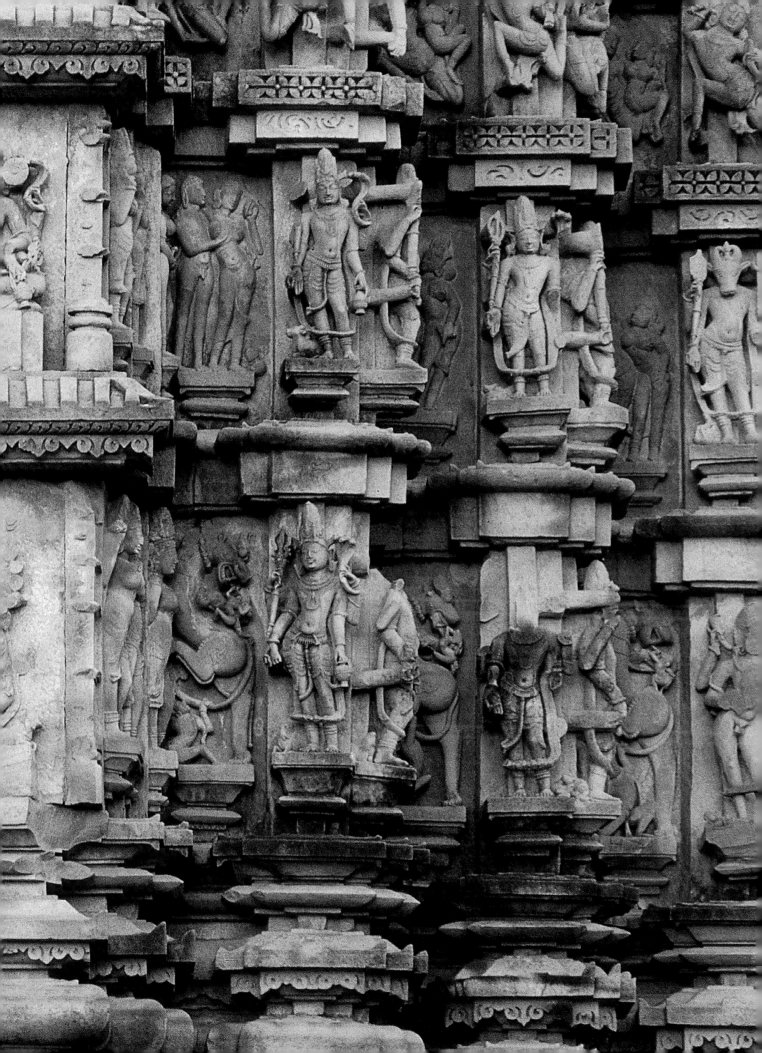

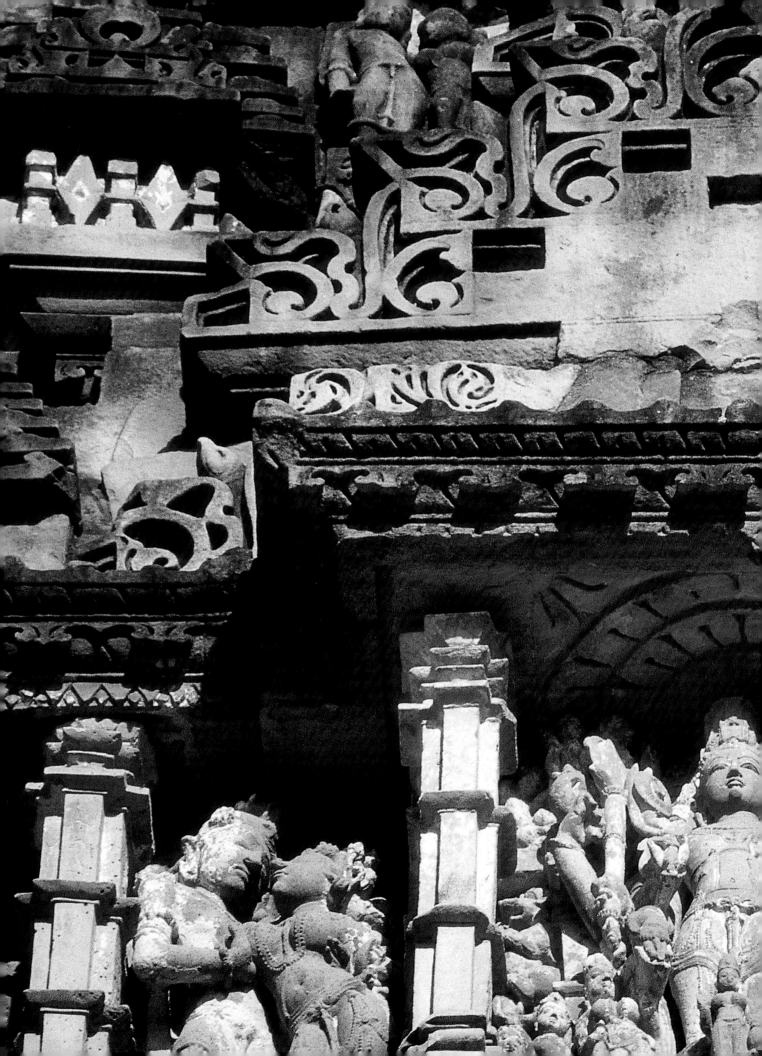

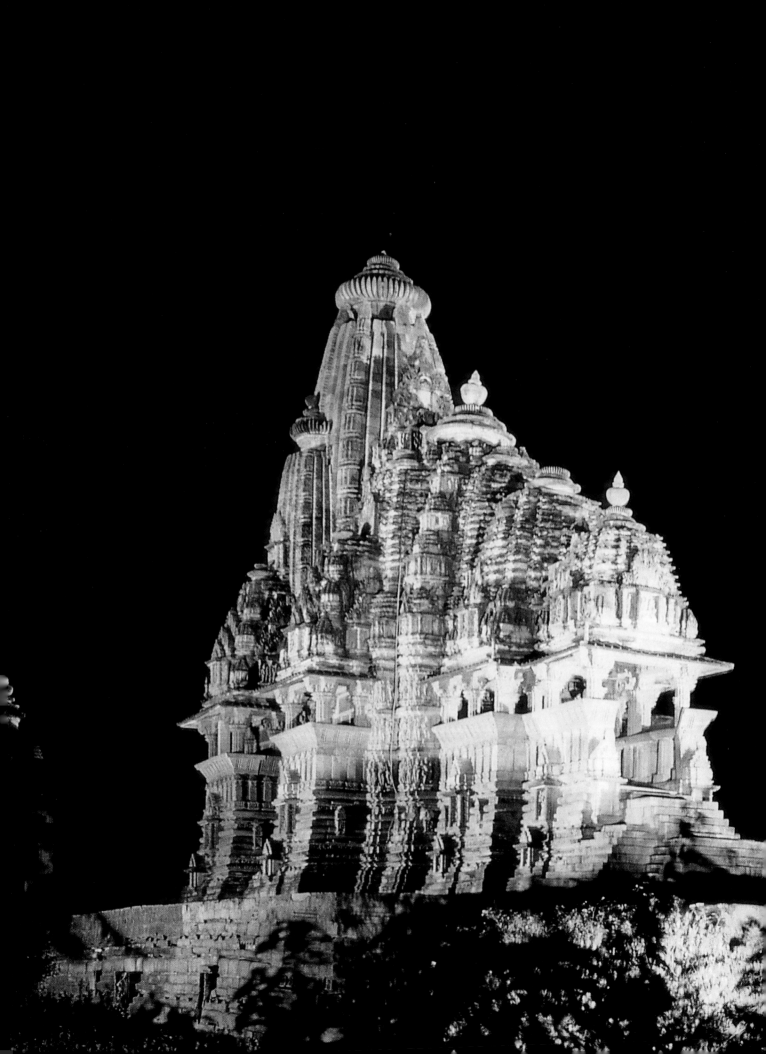

Introduction

A thousand years ago, Khajuraho was a flourishing temple town that lay at the heart of the Chandella kingdom. Mahoba and the fort of Kalinjar were its power centres, but it was in Khajuraho that the greatly chronicled Chandella dynasty chose to build its temples. Today, many of the reasons for choosing Khajuraho as a site for the kingdom's great temple building remain obscure. A small village in the Chattarpur district of Madhya Pradesh, Khajuraho is all but surrounded by wilderness in the midst of a hilly forested belt. When the Chandellas declined in power, Khajuraho for all practical purposes, was lost to the world, its magnificent temples succumbing to centuries of abandonment.

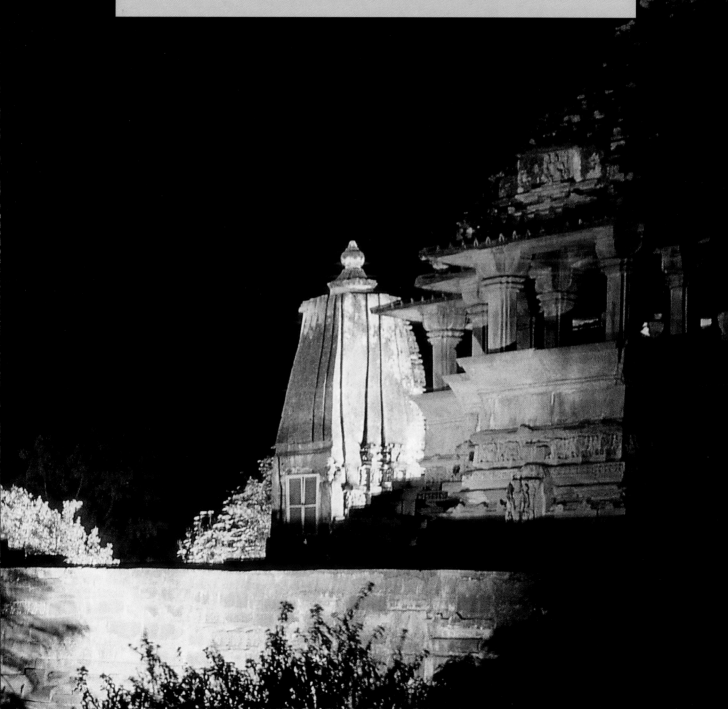

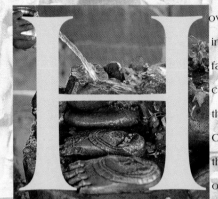

However, nature wrecked less havoc on the temples than invaders might have, and Khajuraho's inaccessibility may, in fact, have been its saving grace. Invading armies never considered it important enough to attack, for Khajuraho lay off the beaten track and surrounded by dense jungles. When the Chandellas were finally consumed by the Delhi Sultanate in the early 14th century, Kalinjar and Mahoba soon became part of the annals of history celebrated for their past, but robbed of the greatness of both their present and future. Khajuraho, of course, literally ceased to be visited only by neighbouring villagers and that too on ritualistic, religious occasions such as *Shivaratri*, the day Lord Shiva is feted as the presiding deity of the temples of Khajuraho.

Rediscovered by the civilised world in 1838 when T.S. Burt, a British engineer, chanced upon the temple ruins. It took more than a century before its relevance to Indian social and art history became apparent, and decades of bureaucratic apathy before it could be brought to the world's attention as a site of historic and tourist importance.

Much more easily reached now, Khajuraho represents the magnificence of medieval temple architecture in India, not least because there are so many of the 85 built, 22 have survived and so grand. Because it lies in the heart of India, far from major towns, Khajuraho has, however, remained unspoiled. There is an airport, true, but it brings in only tourists. The most convenient rail-head is a five hour drive away. The hotels hug the terrain and are resorts rather than highrise. Tourism is its cottage industry, and the small village leads a schizophrenic existence: as a point of meeting for visitors from around the world, while the settlement itself is deliciously medieval. Indeed, its unnatural quietness in the 20th century could help transport you back over many centuries to a time when the temples were the centre of all social and religious activity in the kingdom.

Geologically, the Khajuraho landscape forms part of the Bundelkhand gneiss outcrop. The Ken (ancient Karnavati) river and its tributaries flow through the forested belt with its wildlife and dense greenery. The stone of the upper Vindhyan or Kaimur ranges varies in shades from buff to light pink and was put to use for the marvellous art of Khajuraho's architects and sculptors.

Historically, Khajuraho forms part of a region that has witnessed the rise and fall of some illustrious dynasties. Up to circa 400 BC, the region was included in the Vatsa kingdom; the Mauryas found it important enough to dispatch an Ashokan rock edict at Gujjara, in Datia district.

(preceding page, 6-7): Bell and chain motifs decorate a pillar at Ghantai temple, dating to the end of the tenth century when Khajuraho's temple building activity was at its zenith. (preceding page, 8-9): The western wall of Duladeo temple, part of the Southern Group, shows the extent to which the temples are carved with sculptures, and harmonised in their placement, calling for a high degree of aesthetic and architectural skill. (preceding page, 10-11): Stylised columns, niches and arches were used to designate spaces for important deities such as Surya, the sun god, on the western wall of Vishvanath temple. (preceding page, 12-13): Briefly lit at night, the dramatic silhouettes of the temples bring alive the legacy of the Chandella rulers centuries after they abandoned their temple town.

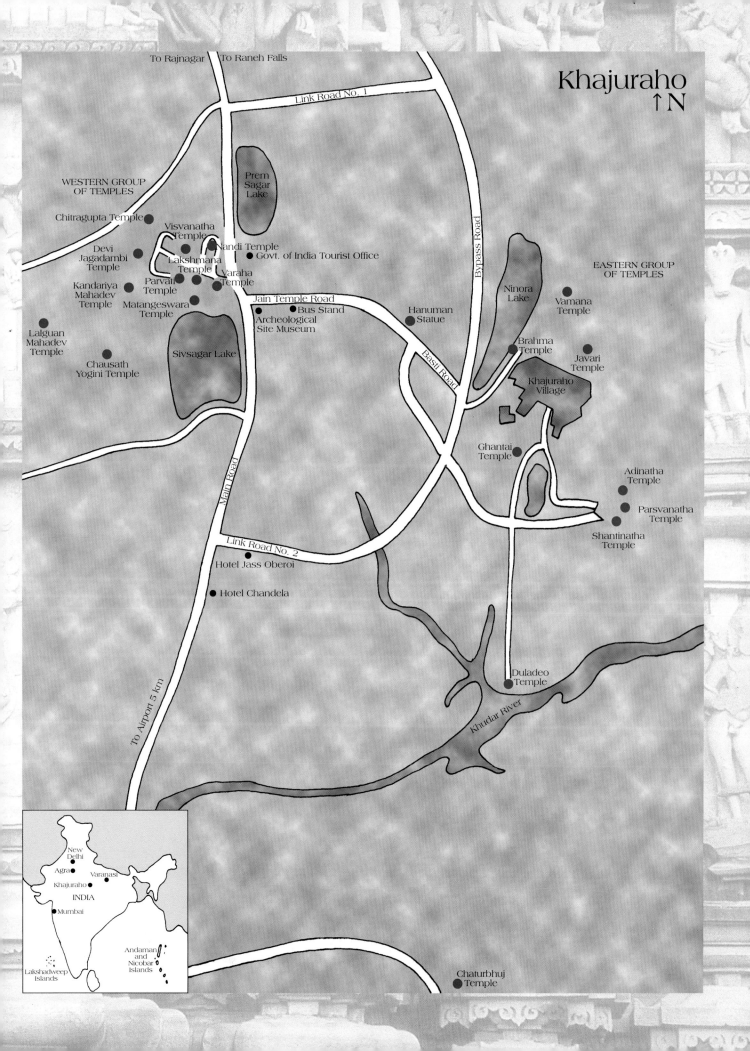

Bharasiva-Nagas, the Vakatakas, the imperial Guptas and the Pratiharas built their empires on and around this land and left their imprint on the cultural canvas of what is known as Bundelkhand. Vestiges of the ancient sculptural and architectural tradition have been found at Bharhut, Bhumara, Nachna and Deogarh. Khajuraho, however, claims only the Chandellas as its sole creators and owes its existence to no other dynasty. Within a span of a hundred years between 950-1050, the Chandellas erected their grand temples. In what art-historian and author Percy Brown finds, "a brilliant episode in the history of Indian temple architecture rather than the progressive course of a concerted movement, representing one of those rare occasions. When religious emotion and unstinted patronage coincided with a flowering of artistic genius to find expression in a group of buildings of the highest aesthetic standard and the utmost significance".

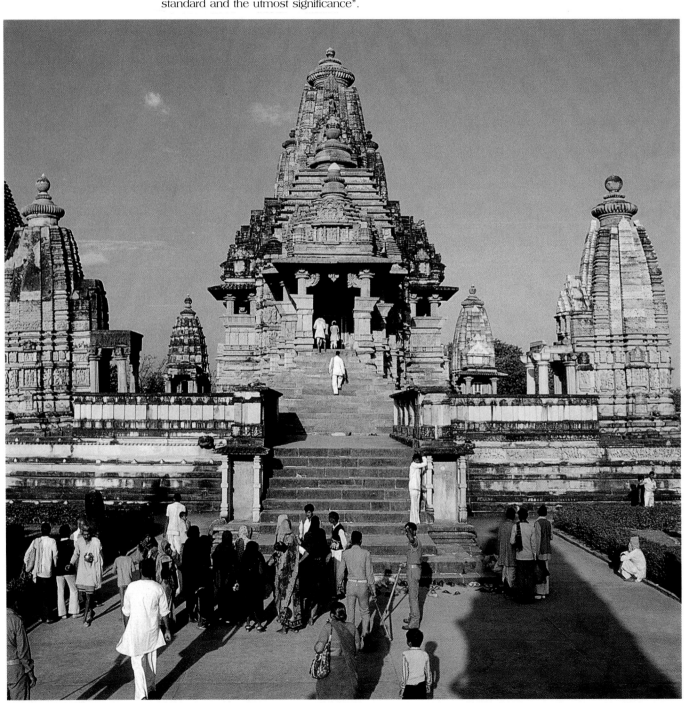

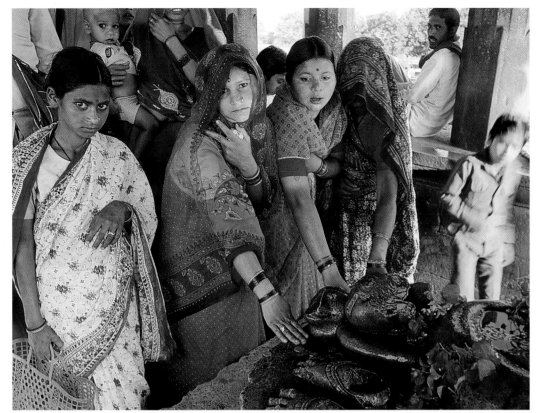

The Chandella land was known as Jejabhukti or Jejakabhukti, with a few other variants. Abu Rihan Al Biruni, who accompanied Mahmud of Ghazni when he sacked the strategic fort of Kalinjar in 1022, mentions the region as Jejahuti in his writings and that Mahoba not Khajuraho, was the capital. Later, Ajaigarh was to be the Chandella, stronghold following the capitulation of Kalinjar. Khajuraho, it appears was the Chandellas' country resort, and a centre of pilgrimage where people of different faiths assembled to offer homage to their gods and practise rituals which had earned it a certain reputation. Ibn Battuta, in 1335, called the place Kajarra and recorded a description thus: "Where there is a great pond about a mile in length near which are temples containing idols which the Muslims have mutilated. In the centre of that pond there are three cupolas in which live a body of the *jogis* (mendicants) who have clotted their hair and let them grow so that they become as long as their bodies and on account of their asceticism their colour had become extremely yellow. Many *Musalmans* follow them in order to take lessons from them. It is said that whoever is subjected to a disease like leprosy or elephantiasis lives with them for a long period of time and is cured by the permission of god." This is the first recorded testimony to the existence of various religious groups including Muslims, at Khajuraho.

History shows that the Chandellas exhibited admirable religious tolerance. In a region where unexcavated mounds indicate early Buddhist settlements, Shaiva, Vaishnava and Jain shrines stand together. These temples show no sectarian difference in their architectural styles or in the choice of images mounted on the outer walls. Dhanga, the greatest of the Chandella rulers, for example, completed the Vaishnava Lakshman temple the construction of which was started by his father Yashovarman, built the Shaivite Vishvanath temple, and gave grants for the erection of the Jain Parsvanath temple.

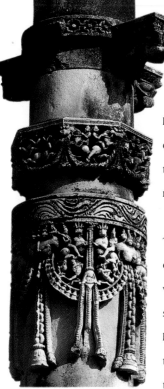

Temple building, however, was not an isolated activity. The Chandella court had renowned poets like Madhava, Rama Nandan, Gadadhara, Jaganika, and the famous dramatist Krishna Misra, author of the classic *Prabodhachandrodaya*, a mirror of contemporary social and religious life. Characteristically, therefore the temples, though religious by nature, have shown a social temperament both in the nature of the sculptural iconography as well as, in being the centre

When the Chandellas slid into historic and social oblivion, Khajuraho too surrendered to its destiny. The jungle grew around the temples and for nearly 500 years after 1309, when Alauddin Khilji wiped out the Chandella power from the land, Khajuraho lay in this unfrequented wilderness. Even then, it was to take another century before conservation work on these temples began. While architects and social historians have marvelled at the temples, the average visitor, it would appear, seems to have been drawn here for the erotic quality of the sculptures, a reputation it ill-deserves. For in the final say, the triumph of Khajuraho is the art that brought temple architect and sculptor together to create forms that remain unparalleled even in the great medieval temple-building annals of India.

(above): Celestial beings crowd the hanging bell columns of Ghantai temple with exquisite detail.
(right): The temples are girdled with bands of sculpture that provide great insight into the life and times during the medieval period, and especially with relation to the way the people were trained in ways of war, and other means of livelihood.
(facing page): Typical of the Khajuraho style of building, Vishvanath temple shares a platform with the Nandi shrine, and contains some exquisite sculptures in the main hall and passageway.

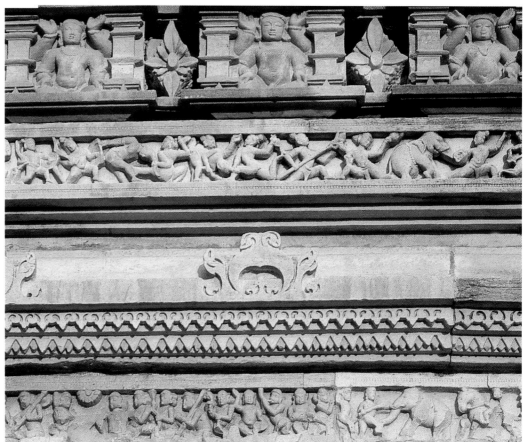

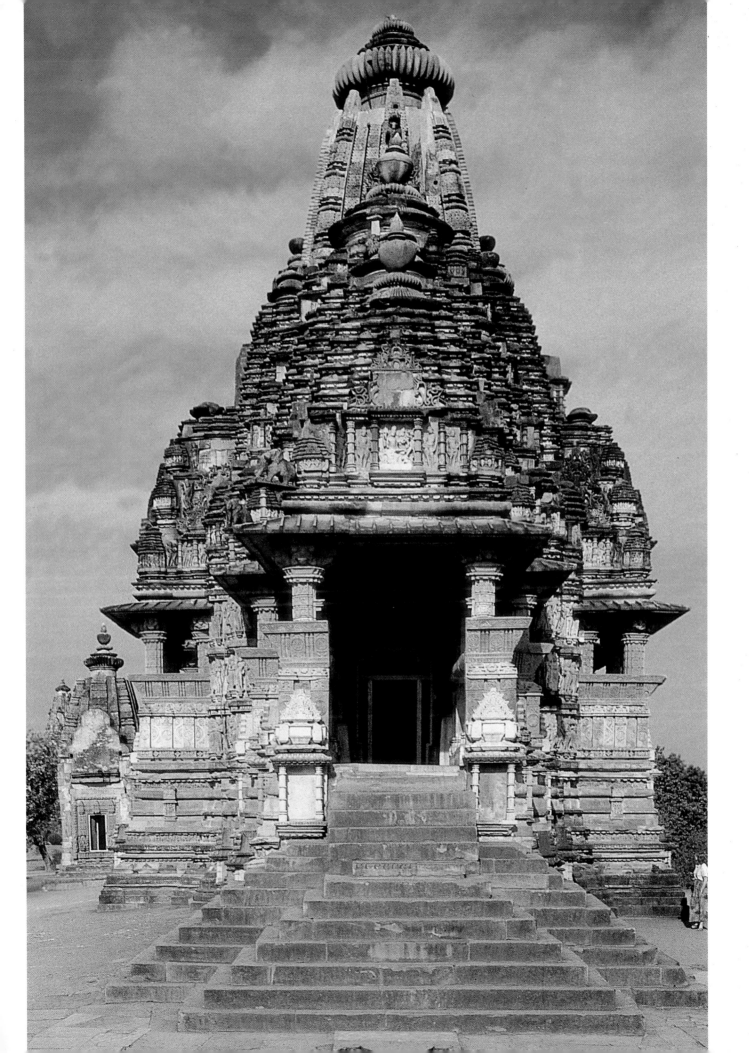

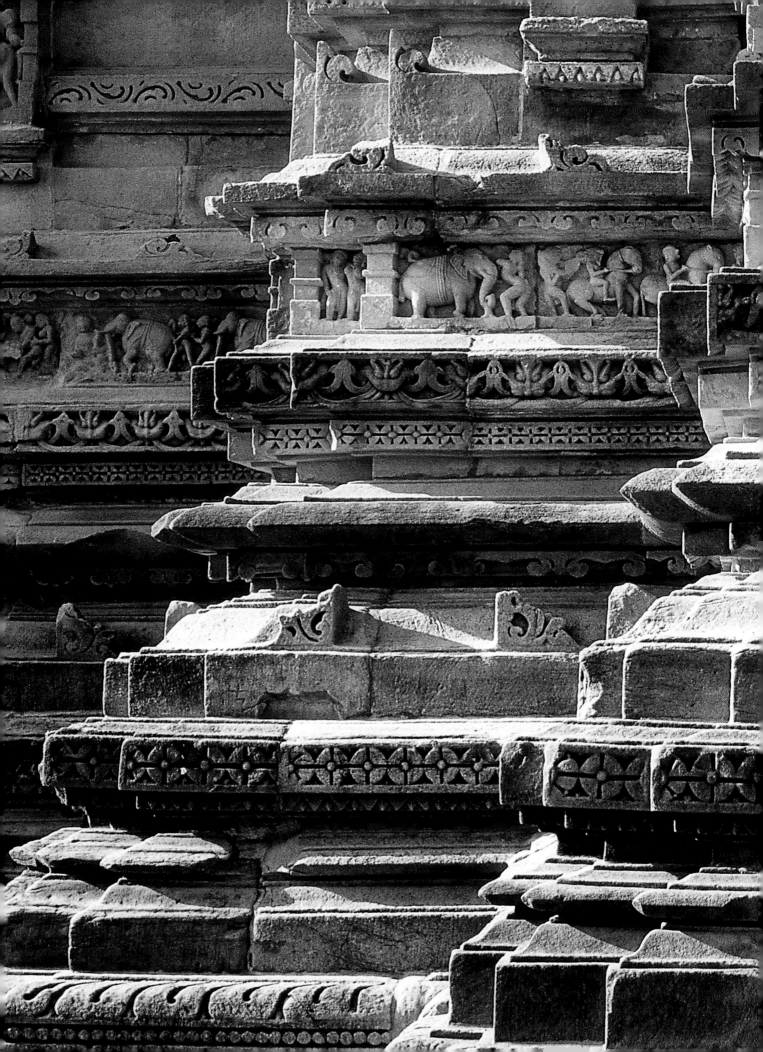

The Chandella Dynasty

Little is known of the Chandellas before their rise to power beyond assumptions that they were local chiefs of humble origin, and were possibly of aboriginal stock. Their journey to kingship began when they wrested power from the Pratiharas, the dynasty that ruled in the region. From then on, the Chandellas went on not only to rule but also became one of the most prominent dynasties from the 10th to the 13th centuries. They extended their influence through aiding rival powers in military exploits, and the acquisition of Kalinjar fort as their stronghold became a symbol of their strength in the Bundelkhand region. It was this that earned them the title of *Kalinjaradipati* or Lord of Kalinjar. Their military capital moved to Ajaigarh in 1203 when they lost the fort to Qutbuddin Aibak, Mohammad Ghori's slave general who founded the Delhi Sultanate. But the three centuries preceding the submission to the Muslim powers formed the glorious period of the Chandellas who combined military strategy with the patronage of art and architecture. The Khajuraho temples are proof of their aesthetic and religious pursuits, even while affairs of the state and military politics took up their time.

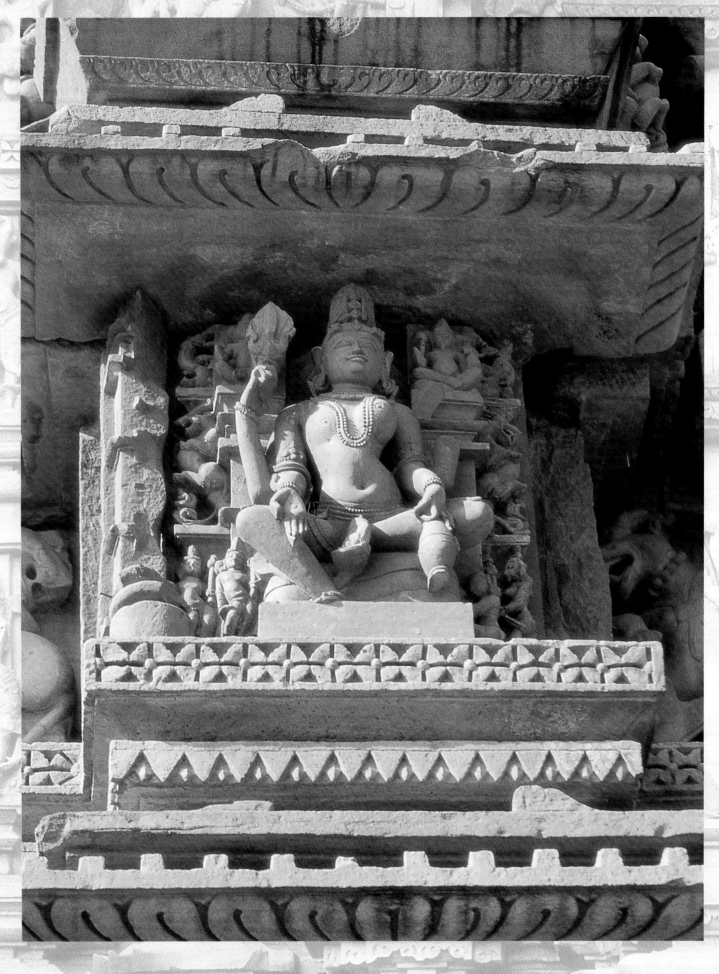

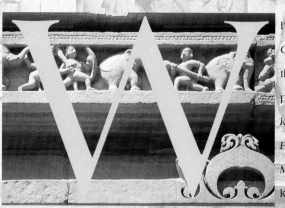

here history fails to trace the origins of the Chandellas, bardic tradition steps in to tell us that the dynasty claims the Moon God as its progenitor, and therefore belongs to the *kshatriya* or warrior races of India. The epic *Prithviraj Raso* has an entire section, the *Mahobakand*, dedicated to the exploits of the kings and warriors in this region, and contains references to the origins of the dynasty. It would appear that Hemvati, a 16-year-old Brahmin widow, was so beautiful that she was seduce by the Moon God when he beheld her bathing in a pond. To condone his act, he promised Hemvati that the child born of their union would be a great warrior and would found a great kingdom and build numerous temples and would rule from Kalinjar.

In due course, and as prophesied, Hemvati gave birth to a son who was named Chandra in honour of his father. As a child, he was groomed by the Moon God, as well as, by celestial deities such as Kubera and Brihspati on administration and politics. Legend records that Chandra killed a tiger single-handedly when only 16, started the task of empire building, and through the annexation of

(below): The Eastern Group's Javari temple stands in splendid isolation, amidst fields. Few visitors take the trouble to visit this exquisite, if small, temple.
(facing page): Sunlight glances off an image of Parvati set in a niche, the shadows and play of light adding a sense of reality to the stone sculpture.
(preceding page): The base wall of the temples consists of a series of tiers, each exquisitely embellished with bands, borders, and motifs, to achieve a look that is as ornamental as it is magnificent.

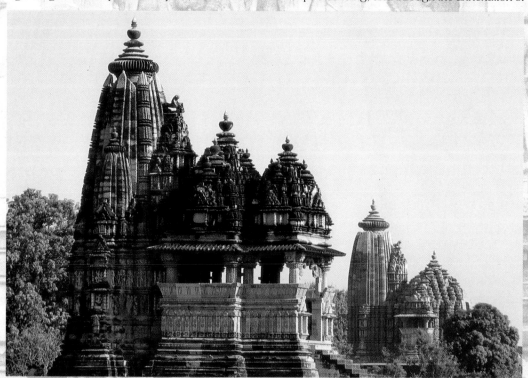

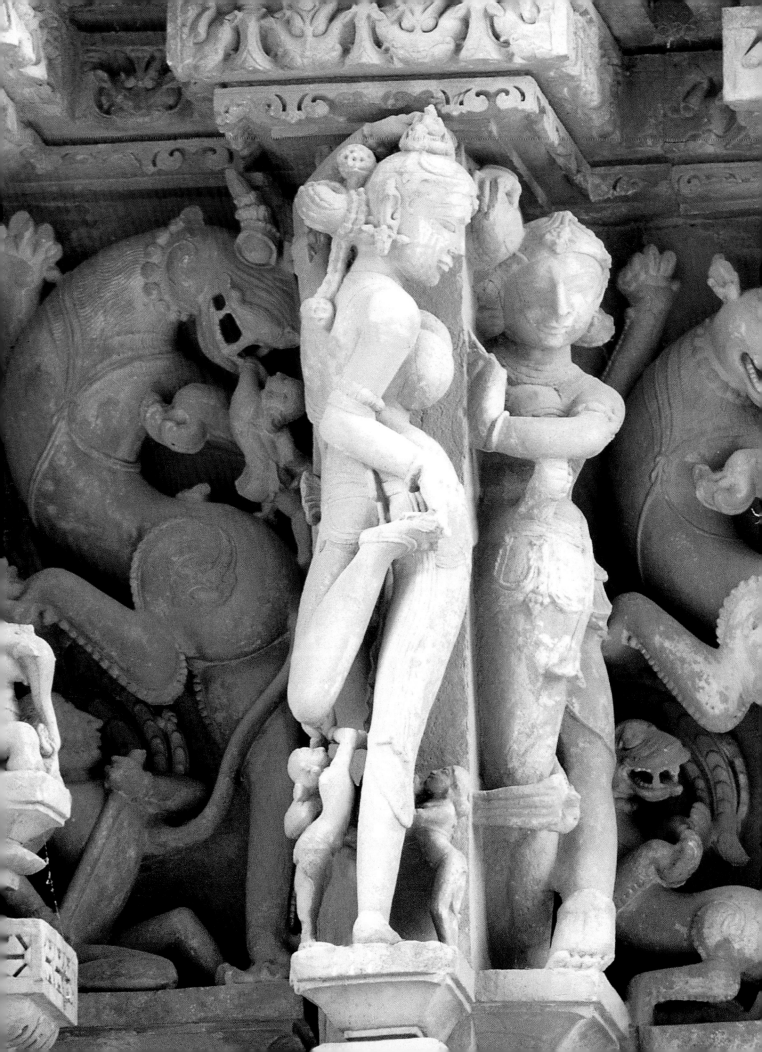

adjoining territories, laid the foundation for the Chandella dynasty. To perform the ritual *Bhanda Yajna*, an act that would condone his mother's sin for bearing a child out of wedlock, Chandra then built the 85 temples in Khajuraho — in four hours, so it is said.

Historical and epigraphic records of the early rulers of the Chandella dynasty are few and do little to justify the great tales of valour and distinction associated with them. Nannuka was the first known Chandella ruler extolled as a great warrior who "playfully decorated the faces of the women of the quarters with the sandal of his fame". He was courageous and won many battles. The exact dates of his rule remain uncertain but it is generally believed to have been in the 9th century when the Chandellas first came into prominence. Nannuka, in fact, might have been the ruler who wrested Mahoba from the Pratiharas.

Vakpati, like his predecessor Nannuka, must have been a powerful chieftain making capital out of the political instability in the region. Constant struggles for supremacy among the three rival powers — the Gurjara Pratiharas, the Rashtrakutas and the Palas of Bengal offered enough opportunities for the Chandellas to seek influence and new territories in the strife-torn political climate. When the Pratiharas were firmly established in power, the Chandellas became their feudatories. Jay*Shakti* and Vijaya*Shakti* consolidated these early territorial gains, and the former named the land after himself — thus Jejabhukti. As feudatories of the Pratiharas, the Chandellas earned a clear political status, albeit as a secondary political power in the region.

Rahilla, who succeeded Vijaya*Shakti*, built several tanks and temples at Mahoba and Ajaigarh, some of which have survived. In fact, Rahilyasagar, a tank in Mahoba, reminds us of the Chandella king, who "never tired (of) the sacrifice of battles".

The Chandellas emerge in a clearer historical perspective with Harsha believed to have ruled 900-925. Rival political powers sought military and matrimonial alliances with the Chandellas. Harsha helped the Pratihara ruler, Mahipala regain Kannauj from the Rashtrakutas. He also married a Chauhan princess while the Kalachuri king Kokkalla I married a Chandella princess. The Chandellas had now become a force to reckon with. Yashovarman, Harsha's son, was a renowned ruler who built the magnificent Lakshman temple at Khajuraho, "the object of attraction for even the inhabitants of heaven", and ruled prior to the consecration of the temple in 953-54. He also acquired Kalinjar from the Pratiharas and thus bolstered his claims as a strong ruler. He remained constantly engaged in battles for territorial aggrandizement and must have caused his adversaries sleepless nights.

Dhanga, the most illustrious of the Chandella rulers, held two strong fortresses — Gwalior and Kalinjar. He was both feared and respected by his enemies and allies. He completely discarded tutelage to the Pratiharas and titled himself Maharajadhiraja. He is also believed to have raided territories in the Deccan. The tremors caused by the invading armies of the Muhammedan forces running through the north-western part of India were heard in the Chandella kingdom. Though never directly attacked by the forces of Mahmud of Ghazni, Dhanga sent his troops to swell the combined forces opposing him in Punjab. This added to his image, making him appear invincible. Dhanga established an efficient bureaucratic machinery and showed remarkable religious tolerance.

(facing page): Flanked by the shardul figures representing the mythical beasts, these celestial beauties from Adinath temple (Eastern Group) symbolise the homage to women paid by the unknown sculptors of Khajuraho.

25

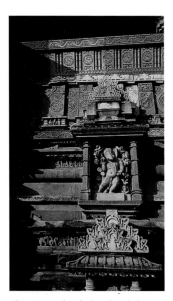

Shiva's son, the elephant-headed, pot-bellied Ganesh is a popular icon, propitiated as a remover of obstacles. In a niche from Kandariya Mahadev temple, Western Group.

He lived for over a hundred years, finally relinquishing his life in the Sangam at Allahabad in 1002. The Chandella kingdom at the time of his death extended all the way between Vidisha and Gwalior, Varanasi and the Narmada.

Ganda, Dhanga's son and successor, was an able administrator but lacked the distinction of a warrior. When *Vidyadhara* succeeded Ganda, the Chandellas faced a direct threat from Mahmud's forces, which had made the invasion of Indian territories an annual excursion for loot and plunder. In 1019, *Vidyadhara* faced Mahmud's army beside a river. He chose to run away under the cover of darkness without raising his sword, leaving behind 580 elephants and an immense booty for easy plunder. The Gwalior and Kalinjar forts invaded by Mahmud in 1022 and at both places the Chandellas placated the enemy by offering huge tributes of riches and elephants. Fortunately, the enemy forces did not destroy much. But what *Vidyadhara* lacked in courage, he more than made up with the construction of Khajuraho's most magnificent temple, the Kandariya Mahadeva.

Vijayapala, who succeeded *Vidyadhara*, could not fight the forces of decline that had set in, nor could he prevent loss of territories and prestige. The Muslim army had left behind the shattered vestiges of Chandella supremacy. The rise of the Kalachuris was yet another factor that contributed to the setback of the Chandella rulers. Fortune smiled once more on the Chandellas when Kirtivarman assumed power and inflicted a crushing defeat on the Kalachuris. He excavated tanks at Mahoba, Chanderi and Kalinjar. The 40 years of his rule (circa 1060-1100) witnessed a revival of Chandella grandeur but his successors lacked any distinction though they did manage to hold the kingdom together without losing any more territories.

The Chandellas were still a prominent political force in 1166 when Parmardi ascended the throne. But two invasions had disastrous results on the Chandella kingdom. Prithviraj Chauhan, the ruler of Delhi, sacked Mahoba and Jejabhukti in 1182-83 isolating the Chandella forces within the confines of Kalinjar fort. The Chauhans were successful in crippling the Chandellas, which is why in 1202, when Qutbuddin Aibak and Iltutmish invaded Kalinjar, Parmardi surrendered and was assassinated by his soldiers for this inglorious conduct. The humbled Chandellas barely managed to cling on to their pride and a much-reduced kingdom.

Trailokyavarman regained Kalinjar from Aibak and retained it till 1233. He also recovered other lost territories so his kingdom lay between the rivers Betwa in the west to the Son in the east, and from Banda and Hamirpur in the north to Panna in the south. He ruled up to 1247. Virvarman, his successor, witnessed the fall of Gwalior, Chanderi and Malwa to Sultan Nasiruddin of the Delhi Sultanate.

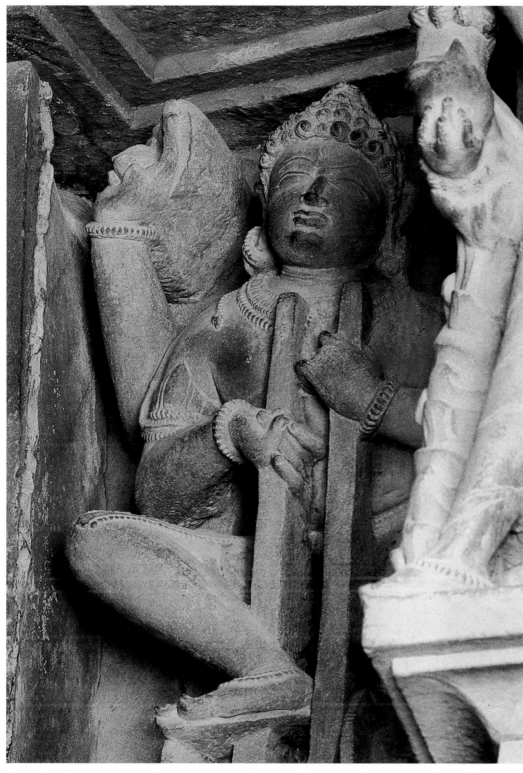

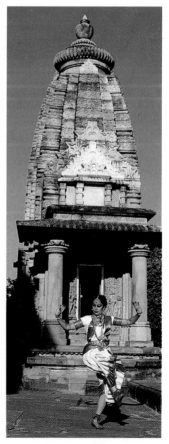

(left): Though principally a Shaivite centre, tales abound from the Ramayana and the Mahabharata, such as this myth of Krishna destroying a chariot. From the interior of the Lakshmana temple, Western Group.
(below): Dancer Sonal Mansingh strikes a pose before a temple. An annual festival of dances is staged in March.

Hammiravarman became ruler in 1290 in the shadow of a devastating attack by the Delhi Sultans. But it was only in 1309 that the forces of Alauddin Khilji finally descended on the Chandella capital to assimilate it in the Sultanate. Nothing was heard of the successors of Hammiravarman after this event.

The Chandellas who had gained a kingdom through grit and determination, proved unable to face the Turkish onslaughts with the courage and valour befitting their status and vaunted claims as warrior-rulers. In the end, they had only their temples to tell of their lost glory.

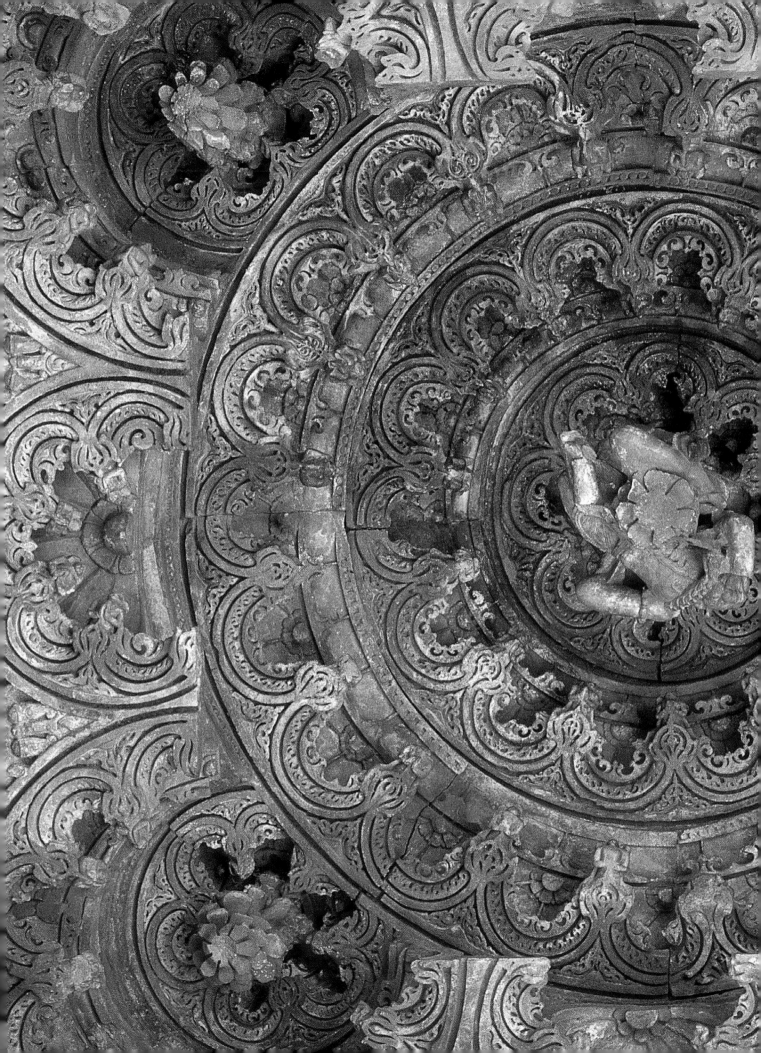

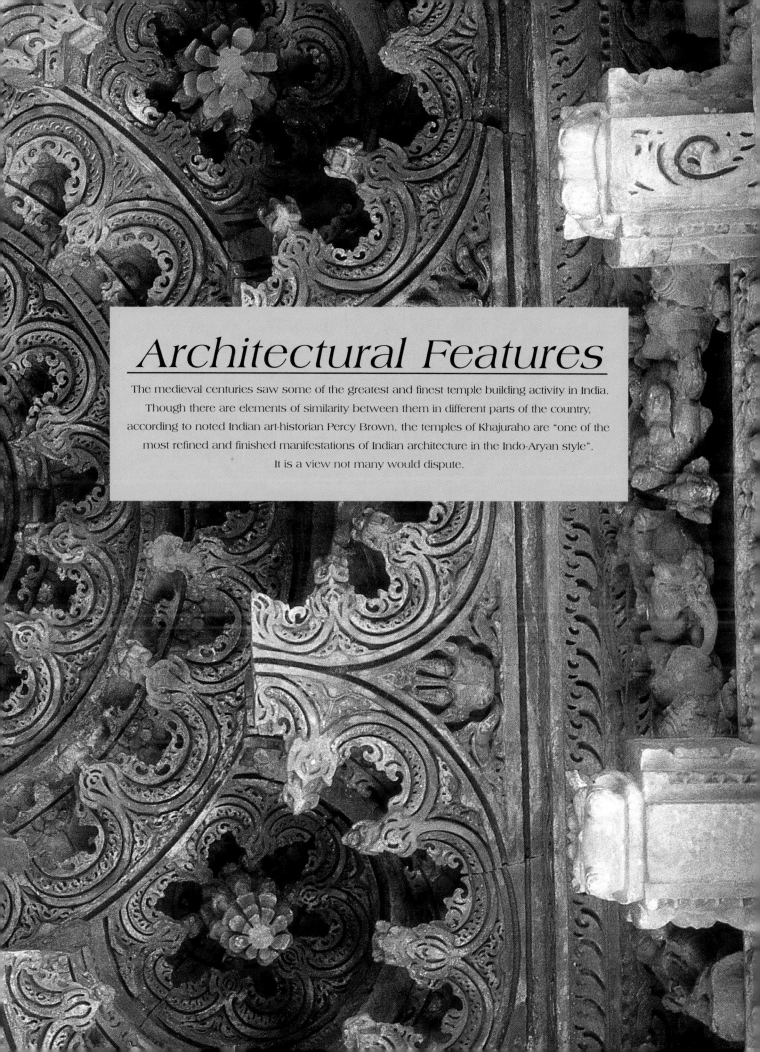

Architectural Features

The medieval centuries saw some of the greatest and finest temple building activity in India. Though there are elements of similarity between them in different parts of the country, according to noted Indian art-historian Percy Brown, the temples of Khajuraho are "one of the most refined and finished manifestations of Indian architecture in the Indo-Aryan style". It is a view not many would dispute.

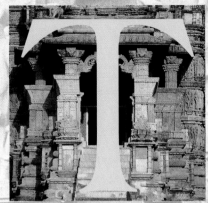

hese temples are dedicated to gods and goddesses of two major religions — Hindu and Jain — and the two Hindu sects, *Shaiva* and *Vaishnava*. In each group, there is a leading shrine, prominent and more lavishly ornamented than the others. The Kandariya Mahadeva is the chief *Shaiva* temple, the Lakshman is *Vaishnava* while the Parsvanath is the biggest Jain temple. However, there is little difference in their architectural style and sculptural decoration that sets them apart. In fact, but for the deity consecrated within the sanctum, it would be difficult to categorise them into three groups.

Chausath *Yogini*, the oldest Khajuraho shrine, is built entirely of granite, while later ones are of buff- or cream-coloured sandstone excavated from the Panna and Ken river banks. Only in the brief transitional phase did the Lalguan Mahadeva and Brahma temples use both granite and sandstone.

Each temple stands on a high terrace to command a view. The smaller temples, in general, have three compartments, namely the *ardha mandapa* (entrance porch), *mandapa* (assembly hall), and *garba griha* (sanctum sanctorum). But the fully evolved Khajuraho temple, of which the Lakshman, Vishvanath and Kandariya Mahadeva are examples, has two additional features: an *antarala* (vestibule) and a *mahamandapa* (transept), together with an ambulatory around the sanctum. These *mandapas* are axially aligned east to west. Structurally, the ground plan of the bigger *mandapas* is in the form of a double Latin cross. The ingenious manipulation of light within the interior creates a feeling of space. The rationally planned *mandapas* are not separate structures but coordinated to form a compact architectural unit. Internally, the sanctum is the central point and all structural lines lead towards it.

The accentuated verticality of the whole structure is the most striking feature of the Khajuraho temples. All eyes are drawn to the *amalak* (a ribbed ring of stone) and *kalasha* (auspicious water pot) crowning the *shikhara*, the spire over the sanctum. To this end, all the structural features are patterned to aid the rising crescendo of the *prasada*. The rich and diverse series of mouldings on the plinth of the structure resemble tiers of horizontal ribs, lightening the burden, as it were of the breathtaking monumentality of the whole structure. The jagged form of the mouldings imparts a vibrant quality to the edges.

The structure above these mouldings is the most important portion enclosing the *mandapas* and the sanctum. The temple, characteristically has no facade and the four walls do not meet at right angles. The walls are of varying thickness, depending on their distance from the sanctum. They have

(facing page): The entrance to the Kandariya Mahadev temple with its torana archway is representative of the effect the architects wished to create, of a rising crescendo of peaks resembling the Himalayas. (preceding page):The ceilings of the entrance porch of the temples were often magnificently carved, as in the Parsvanath temple, the pillars supporting a circular pattern set with sculptured panels on the sides.

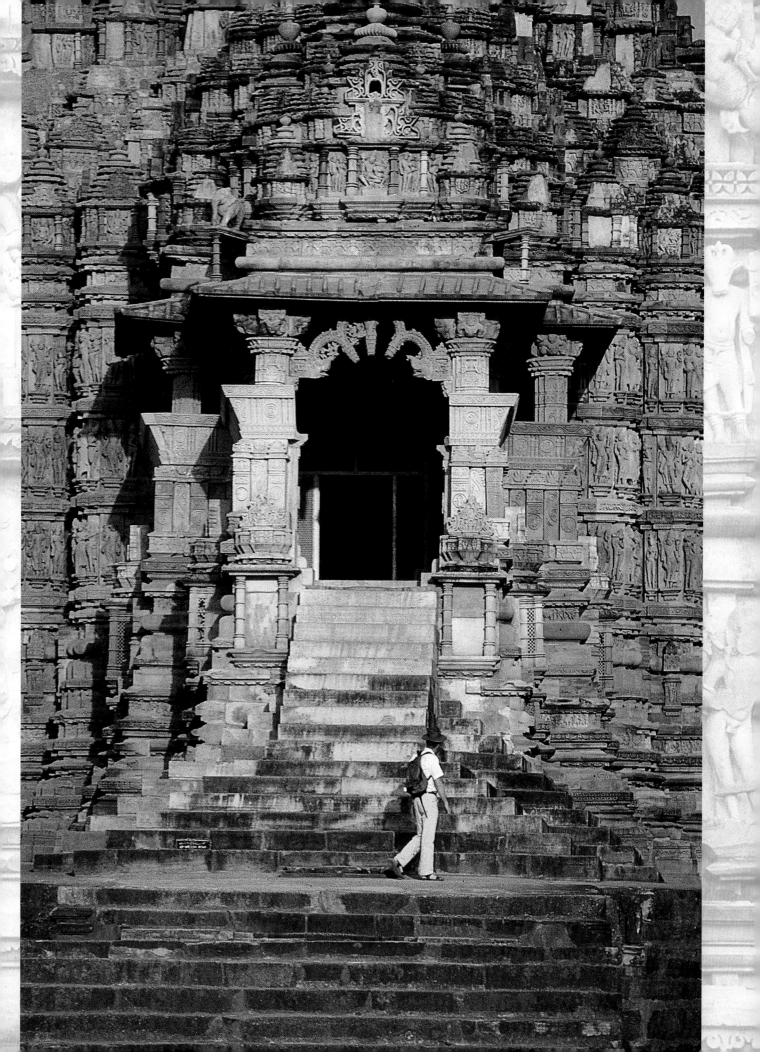

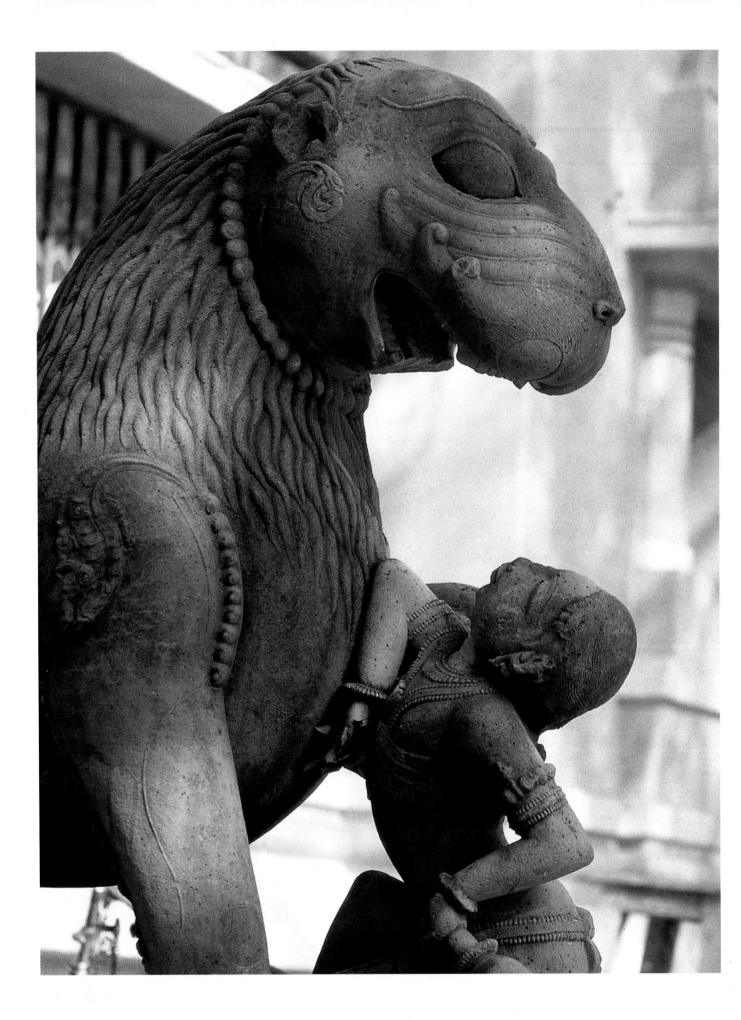

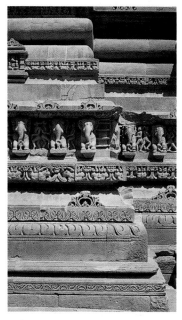

(above): Elephants are often used as posts to support successive tiers of the walls, and scenes from everyday life are cleverly juxtaposed into the niches, as in the Lakshmana temple. (facing page): The leit motif at Khajuraho is the recurring image of a young warrior grappling with a lion-headed shardul, taking its genesis from the origins of the clan which had the dynastic head fighting with lions in the jungles of Bundelkhand.

a number of offsets, projections and recesses. In the space between these projected buttresses and offsets are space, volumes and rhythms of graded light and shade. In an ingenious manner, the architect has introduced his voids consisting of a horizontal range of window openings, projected balconies with seats and wide eaves, allowing sufficient light into the interior and relieving the exterior of structural monotony. These canopied windows throw a dramatic shadow over the wall surface and, as Percy Brown observes, "There are few more attractive conceptions in the field of Indian architecture than these lovely balconied openings, and few either structurally or aesthetically more appropriate to the purpose."

In human terms, the temple can be defined with the *adisthana* (base) representing its legs, the *jangha* (mid-portion) as its waist, and the *shikhara* as its head. The *jangha* consists of double- or triple-bands of sculpture girdling the edifice. These friezes depict Hindu gods and goddesses, celestial beauties, erotic couples and the *sardula* (a mythical beast, usually depicted as half-lion, half-horse) in the recesses. In fact, in view of the high frequency of their appearance, the *sardula* images probably number the highest though erotic couples or *mithunas* too have an extraordinary presence. This magnificent statuary contributes vibrancy to the fabric of the temple, making them pulsate with energy. The splendour of their form is the most remarkable feature of the sculpture decorating the surface of the exterior. These bands of figural sculpture strike a perfect balance between horizontal and vertical volumes.

The roofs over the *mandapas* stand graded one higher than the other, leading the eye to the inevitable summit of the *shikhara*. The roof structure shows a steady change from the early pyramidal form to the dramatically soaring *shikhara* of the later fully evolved temples. The pyramidal superstructure is reserved for roofs over the *mandapas* in front of the curvilinear *shikhara*. Stylistically, the smaller temples without transepts around the sanctum and without *urushringas* clustering around the *shikhara* form the other less representative group of temples at Khajuraho.

It is the soaring *shikhara*, not really of any staggering height but of impressive proportions pulled upward through some inner, instinctive urge which is so characteristic of the temples at Khajuraho.

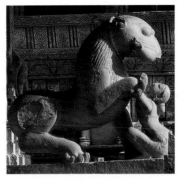

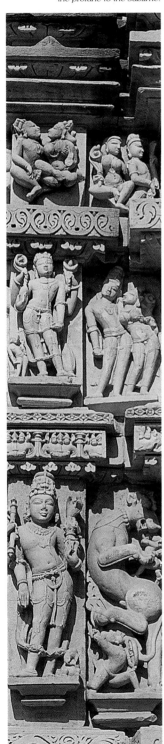

Within the interior, this upward surge is maintained by the rising of floors of *mandapas* leading to the sanctum. To add to the impression of increasing height are the projected buttresses which finally merge into the *urushringas* which are the Khajuraho architect's "most remarkable structural innovation". The *shikhara* emerges out of the heap of *urushringas* in a spectacular finish not unlike the summit of Mt. Kailash rising above the lesser peaks. The curvature of these *shikharas* is compelling. The whole superstructure is, as Benjamin Rowland observes, "a rising crescendo of curves, the curves of the lesser turrets and the ribs of the main tower having their own points of intersection and yet leading inevitably to the *amalak* that at once crowns and girdles the whole". The Kandariya Mahadeva temple has the most magnificent *shikhara* with a great number of *urushringas* clinging to it — truly the most spectacular achievement of the Khajuraho architect. The verticality of the *shikhara* is considerably enhanced by the use of forms representing the cosmos within the larger cosmos in rhythmic repetition such as the *chaitya*-window motifs forming a mesh over the *shikhara*. Non-figurative sculpture, used in overlapping series, and a profusion of pinnacles punctuated by ribs, slots and flanges — all multiplying in profusion — create the "crystallised rhythm" of architecture.

The body of the *shikhara* takes its inward plunge at the neck (*griva*) where it is fitted with the sacred motifs of *amalak* and *kalasha*. The *amalak* crowns the invisible shaft rising from the sanctum below, and is surmounted by the *kalasha*. The *amalak* in the shape of a cogged rim and a ring stone or an indented wheel symbolises the passage to heaven. The *kalasha* contains the qualities of the gods and the *soma* (nectar) which as in the human nervous system crowns the body. The temple is a microcosmic replica of the Cosmic Man (*Mahapurusa*).

The whole body of the temple is the house of god, and from the plinth to the summit of the *shikhara* is, in architectural terms, the manifestation of his divine form. The terrace on which the temple stands provides enough space for circumambulation. This is not meant for admiring the statuary so much as to acquire an awareness of god's divine presence. The visitor becomes "the outermost perimeter to the building" as he moves around in the unrealised presence of the divine.

The interior of the temple is reached through the *ardha mandapa* from where the presiding deity in the *garba griha* is only vaguely visible. The floors of these *mandapas* are graded to rise to the highest level just below the door to the sanctum where a single or double *chandrashila* (moonstone) forms the last step. The pillars in the interior are superbly ornamented and carry marvellous sculptural wealth. The brackets over the pillar capitals are overlaid with figures of grotesque dwarfs and the ubiquitous *Surasundaris* or celestial beauties. Most of these superb sculptures have remained in the

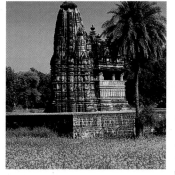

(left): The small but exquisite Javari temple, Eastern Group, is dedicated to Vishnu and has an entrance porch consisting of carved crocodiles.
(below): The placement of niches creates a spatial depth within the ambit of the facade of walls.

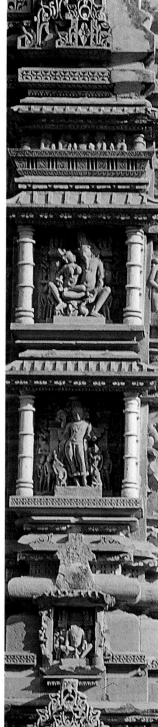

dark for centuries and, except for an occasional curious visitor, few look especially for them.

The ceilings in the interior carry some ingenious designs. The square framework of the architraves is first turned into an octagon and then into a circle to support the ceilings. As per Hindu thought, Vishwakarma — the architect of the gods — gave the first ornament of the square, representing space, to the banner of Indra. Brahma and Shiva gave the circle, representing time. The Chandella architect charted the course of the universal dimension of time within the specific dimension of limited space, reconciling obliquity and inequality to "locate the cosmic girdles of time inside the square". The stone panels were individually finished and later fitted into their proper position to form what looks like a swirling pattern of circles and semi-circles. The workmanship on the stone forms as filigree of breathtaking perfection.

The doorway to the sanctum is the most exquisitely ornamented portion of the interior. On the top of the lintel is carved the image of the presiding deity flanked by smaller images of the attendant deities. In this respect, as Stella Kramrisch observes, "the door is God through whom man enters into the presence of the Supreme Principle which is established in the *garba griha*". Figures of the river goddesses Ganga and Yamuna are sculpted at the base of the two supporting columns. The door symbolises the passage from the mundane to the spiritual, from the temporal to the eternal.

The *garba griha* is a small, square and dark structure bereft of all ornamentation, built in the image of the womb, or the cave, which is the sacred residence of the gods. The energy radiating from the centre of the *garba griha* lends potency to the images of various gods and goddesses on the north, west and south sanctuary walls. The eight deities, the guardians of the eight directions (*Dikpalas*), hold cardinal positions on the temple structure, which is only a symbol of the cosmos. The east-west axis on which the various structural components of the temple are aligned, provides a straight passage to god. The *amalak* and *kalasha* crowning the *shikhara* are precisely in line with the centre of the *garba griha* thus forming an invisible shaft, the core of the transcendental power. The *garba griha* compartment "is the *vastupurusa*, the place of all the gods".

Elaborating upon the symbolic significance of the temple structure, Stella Kramrisch observes: "Its substance and shape (*akriti*) is *Prakriti*, the primordial nature of the world, its images which mirror the course of the world (*samsara*) give liberation. Its total form is the seat (*prasada*) of the Supreme Spirit." The Khajuraho temple, like all Hindu temples, is "the monumental embodiment of the *Purusa*, the Essence, it is the form of Consciousness itself". Every single stone used on the temple structure is thus imbued with the divine spirit, and the holy structure is not only the house of god but god itself.

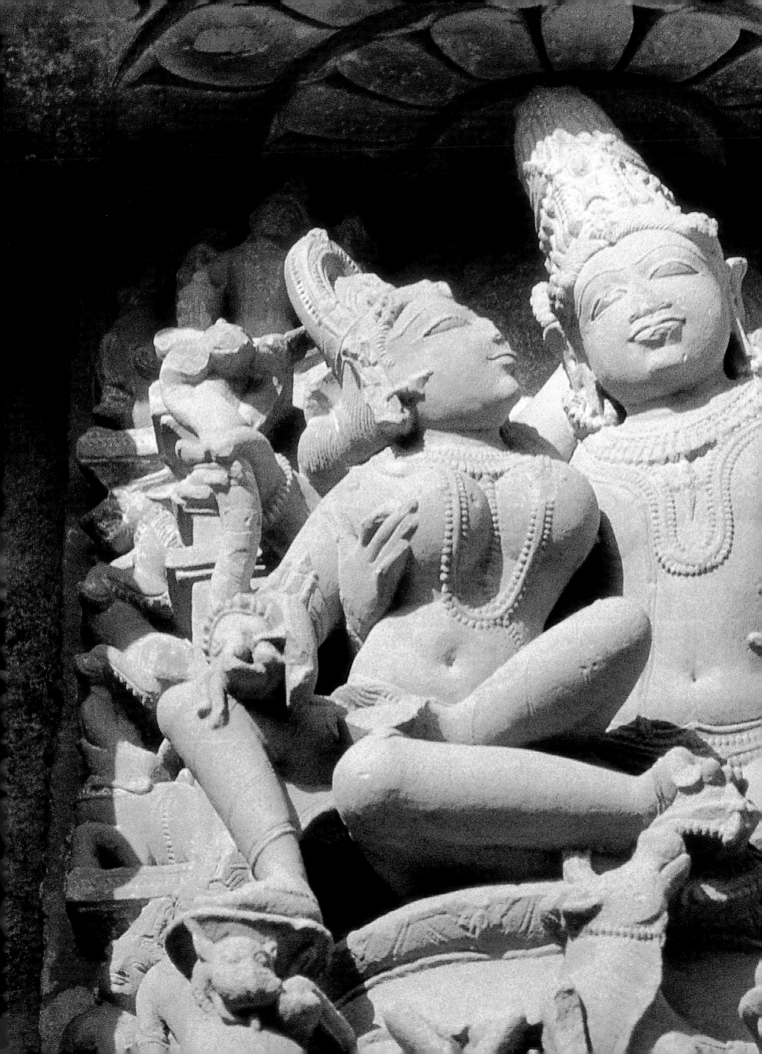

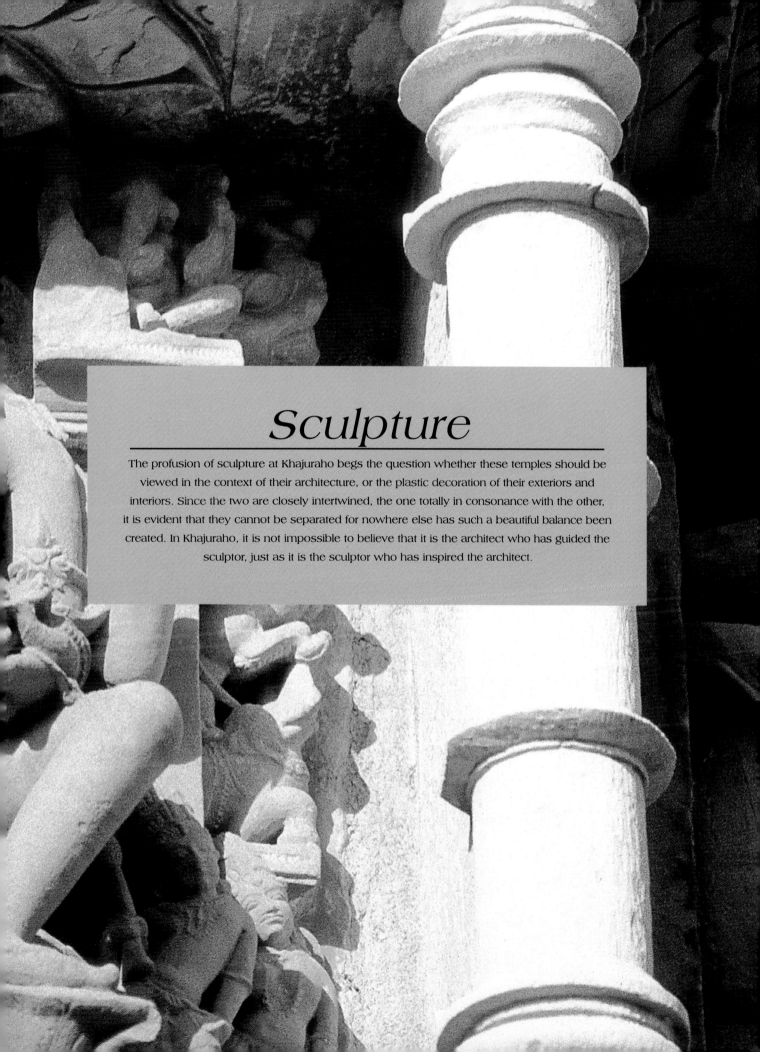

Sculpture

The profusion of sculpture at Khajuraho begs the question whether these temples should be viewed in the context of their architecture, or the plastic decoration of their exteriors and interiors. Since the two are closely intertwined, the one totally in consonance with the other, it is evident that they cannot be separated for nowhere else has such a beautiful balance been created. In Khajuraho, it is not impossible to believe that it is the architect who has guided the sculptor, just as it is the sculptor who has inspired the architect.

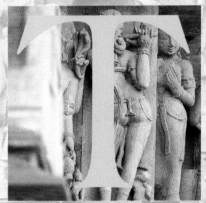

The most striking aspect of the sculptured walls is not just the profusion but the preponderance of the human figure on the body of the structure. From the plinth to the summit of the *shikhara*, from the entrance porch to the top of the pillars in the interior and in the circumambulatory passage around the sanctum, the visitor finds himself looking at a grand procession of gods and goddesses, attendant deities, celestial beauties and dancers — each carved with consummate skill. The Lakshman, Vishvanath and Kandariya Mahadeva temples, in particular, have "a pageantry of forms coalescing with the fabric of the temple and growing out of it, like plants towards the sun", according to writer Stella Kramrisch. This visually three-dimensional sculpture is the most outstanding exhibition of temple architecture and sculpture in India.

The basic sculptures can be classified into the following categories: cult images of gods and goddesses, demi gods, attendant deities and celestial beauties, animals and scenes from ordinary life.

(right): The shardul was often placed at the entrance of the shrines, or on their platforms, to perpetuate the Chandella legend.
(facing page): A celestial dancer surmounts the ceiling of a temple, her necklaces and girdles an excellent representation of the jewellery then in vogue.
(preceding page): Shiva and Parvati are the residing deities of Khajuraho, and many of the great works of sculptural art are dedicated to their sublime love, tales of which are recounted in Hindu legends and myths.

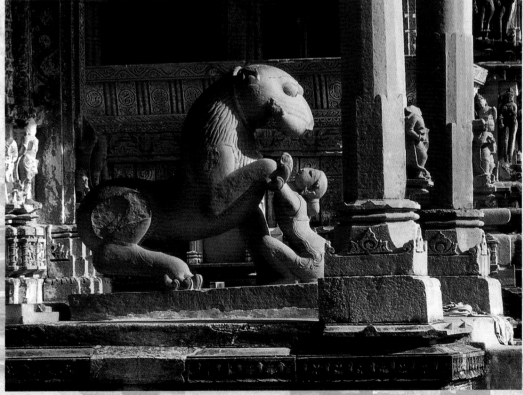

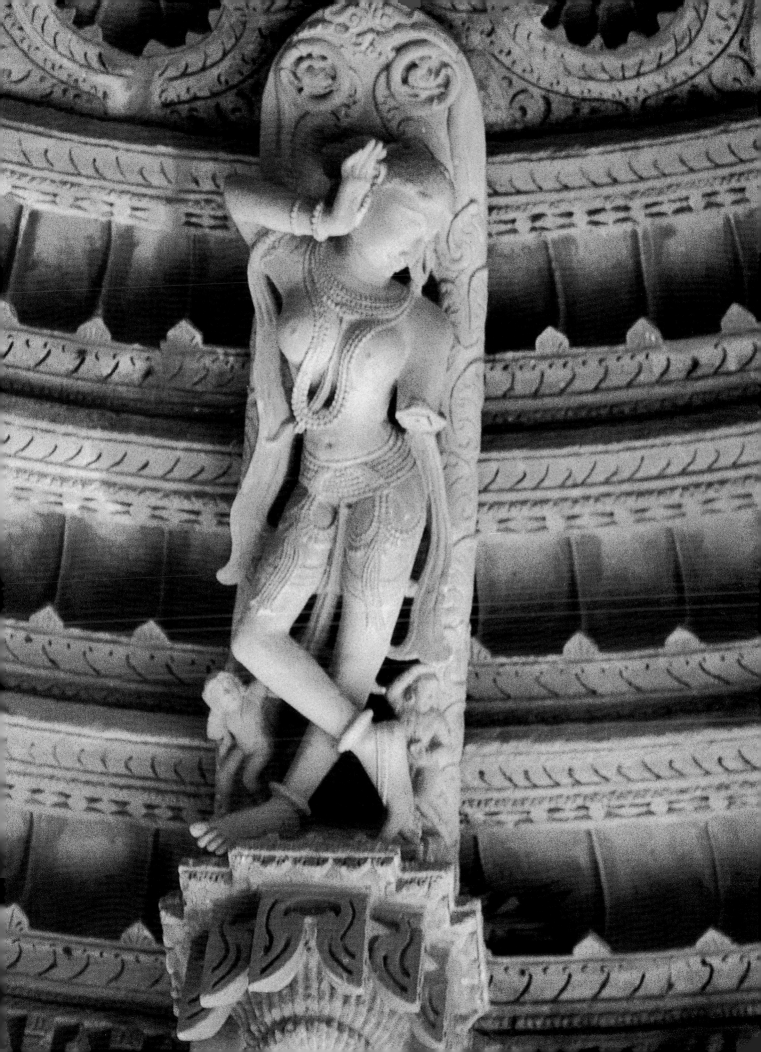

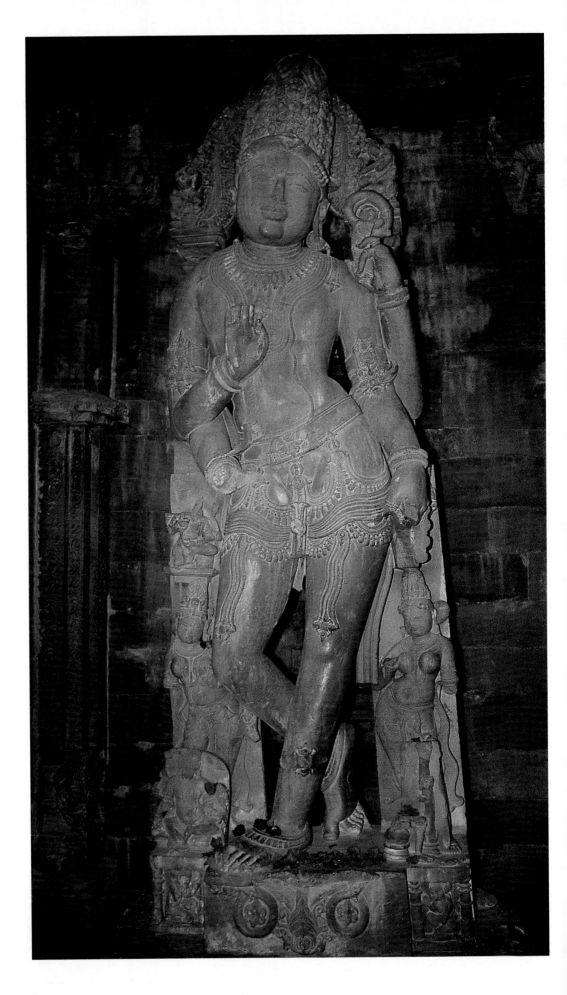

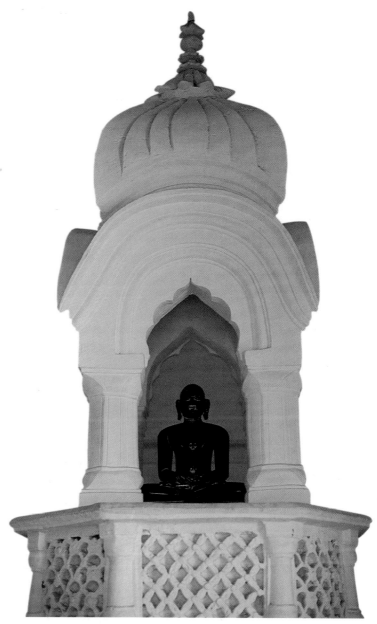

The cult images of gods and goddesses, sculpted almost completely in the round, are meant exclusively to aid devotional concentration by man. These images have been made in strict conformity with canonical and iconographical prescriptions regarding their size, attributes and posture. The numerous images of Shiva, Vishnu, Surya and the Jain Tirthankaras have been flawlessly executed, highlighting their quiet dignity, composure and transcendental serenity. They are distinguished by their rigid, erect stance, surrounding nimbus and the presence of attendant gods and minor deities on the back slab.

The most outstanding of these cult images is the 9 ft high Shiva Dakshina*Murti* at the Chaturbhuja temple. The image, four-armed and splendidly crowned stands on a pedestal on the sunken floor of the sanctum. This is Shiva in his rare form as the supreme teacher. The *tribhanga* (triple curved) posture has a benign presence and charm accentuated by a faint smile. The rich jewellery, garlands and a scarf cover the slender figure. The *makara-torana* behind the crowned head evokes later Chola images.

(above): The Eastern Group of temples is almost totally dedicated to the Jain tirthankaras within the sanctum, though the iconograpy on the walls was usually secular. (facing page): The Dakshinamurti Shiva in the sanctum of the Chaturbhuj temple is four-armed, and the largest sanctum idol in Khajuraho.

The multitudinous deities at Khajuraho include various incarnations of Vishnu, *Matrikas* and *Dikpalas*, mostly depicted with their consorts. Scriptural denial of inventiveness to sculptors renders these figures monotonous in posture. The composite images of Hari-Hara Pitamaha or Dattatreya, Hari-Hara Hiranyagarbha (Surya with the features of the Trinity), and a six-headed, four-legged, twelve-armed Sadasiva combining features of Brahma and Vishnu are in a distinctive class of their own.

Images of the attendant and familial deities are identifiable through their rich crowns, individual mounts and hand-held attributes. Invariably, these images wear a diamond on their chest, and a rich garland of knee-length. The Parsvanath and the Devi Jagdamba temples have a rich galaxy of such divine couples.

(right): This image of Shiva and Parvati has come to represent the high quality of sculptural work in Khajuraho, the art evident in the shared bond the sculptor has so evidently been able to communicate.
(far right): A four-legged image of Shiva from the interior of the Kandariya Mahadev temple.
(facing page): An iconic representation of Yama, the god of death, from the Devi Jagdamba temple, Western Group.

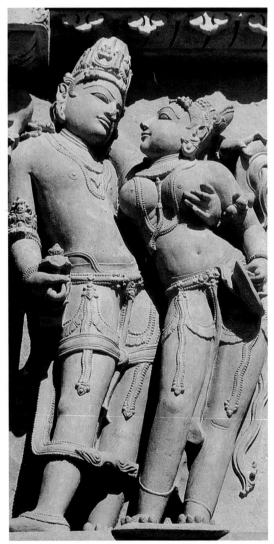

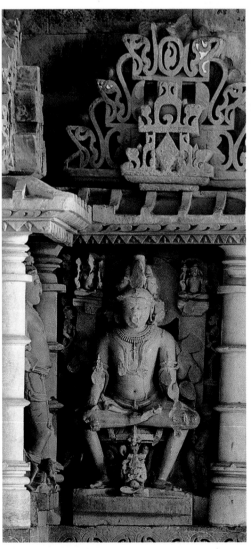

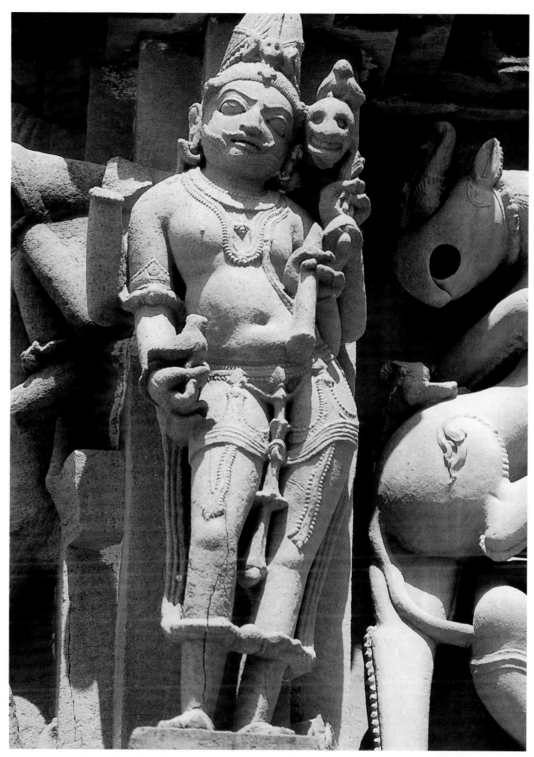

The less divine figures of *ganas* (cherubs), *gandharvas* (celestial musicians) and *vidyadharas* (flying angels) have received the sculptors' lavish attention. The movement in these still figures is captivating. The *vidyadharas* attend on the gods, flying or hovering above them, carrying garlands, sporting a sword or staff. The *gandharvas* are the divine musicians depicted in graceful, aerial postures propelled, as it were, by the "power of levitation inwardly experienced through breath". The *ganas* are sprightly, frolicking in the air around the gods, armed with scimitars and swords, doing duty as guardian angels. Composed solely of light and air, their bodies are unencumbered with the weight of flesh. The Duladeo temple contains the largest number of *gandharvas*, *vidyadharas* and *ganas*.

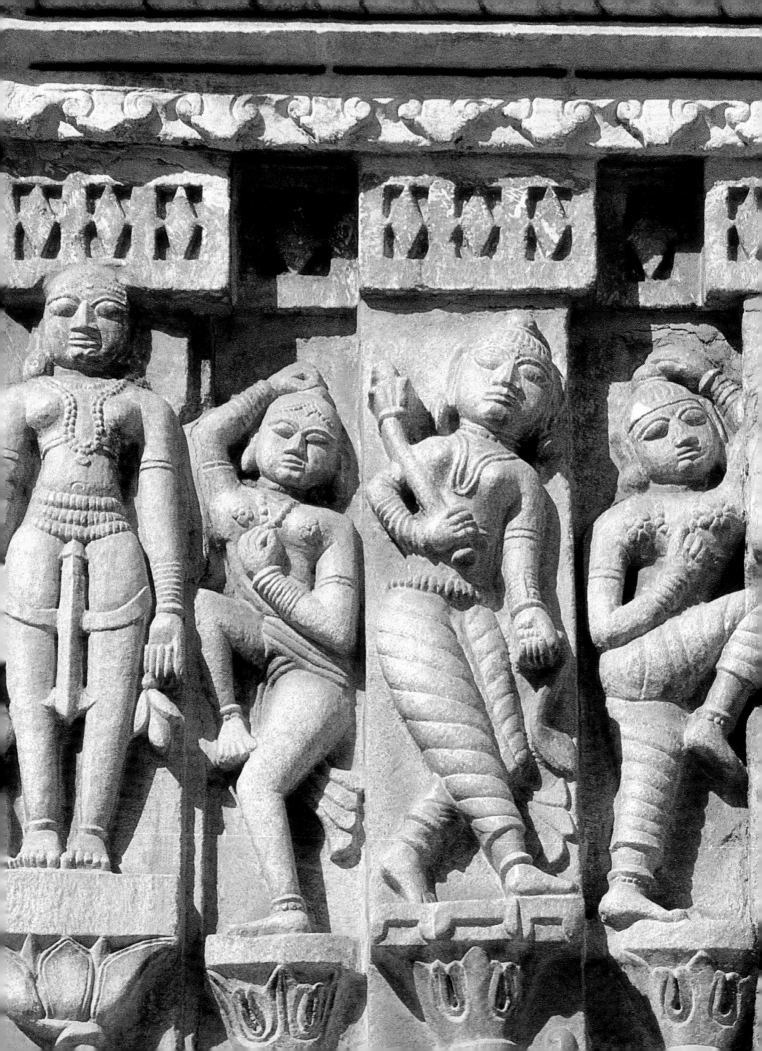

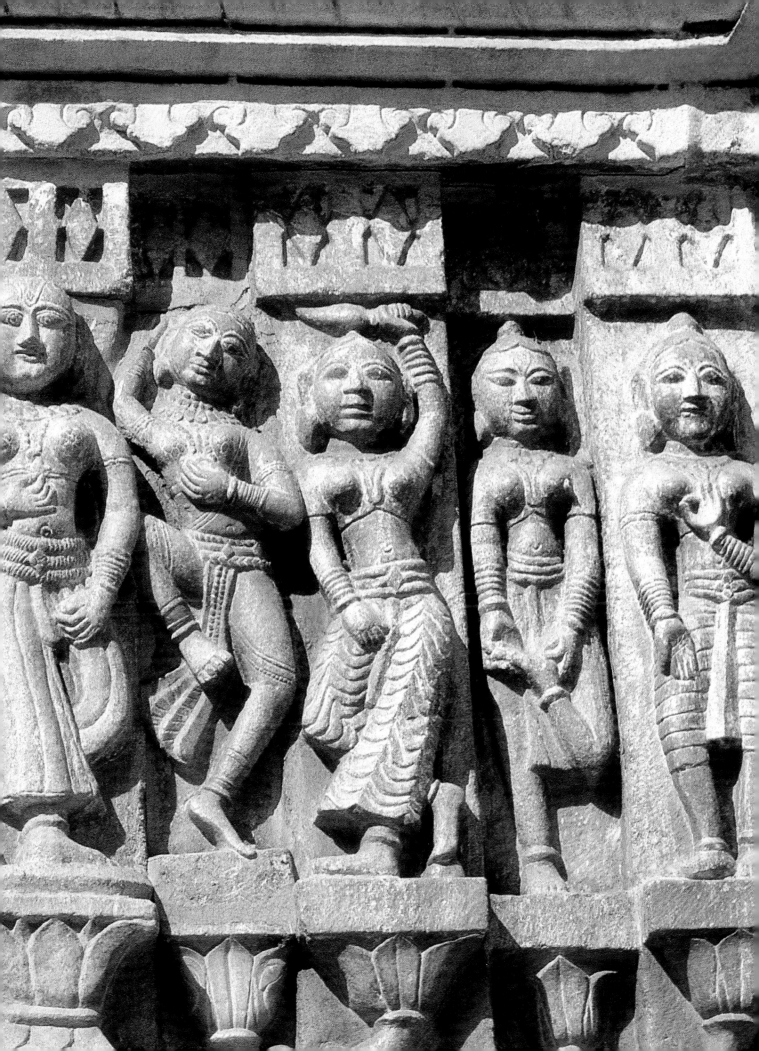

Among the largest body of work to be found here is images of eternally young women, enchanting forms of the primordial, life-giving energy, *Shakti*. *Surasundaris* (celestial beauties), *Nayikas* (beautiful women), *Shalbhanjikas* (tree goddesses) blooming with the nubile charms of perpetual youth flank the images of gods. Their ample physical attributes, seductive postures and sensuous appeal add to their immense attraction. This is the company promised to man on ascending the portals of heaven. The *jangha* of the temple is but a temporary residence for these divine enchantresses, providing a brief view of the pleasures of heaven. The *Apsaras* are the symbols of the cosmic powers. They assist the contemplative and passive nature of man, and their role in purifying the mind of man is vital.

The sculptures depict these celestial beauties in self-absorbed pursuits the moods ranging from occupations of beautifying themselves to admiring themselves in the mirror, applying kohl to the eyes, painting their feet, playing with pets, writing letters, removing thorns from their feet, dancing... Shobita Punja, an author who has opened up a new viewpoint on the reasons for the building of the Khajuraho temples to celebrate Shiva's wedding with Parvati, explains the presence of these damsels noted for their mimetic quality, perennially engrossed in some activity. When Shiva's marriage procession entered the city, she writes, the womenfolk ran to see the Lord: "What the artists at Khajuraho have captured is that single dramatic moment when human beings become aware of the presence of god, an everlasting moment of joy and wonder." This may well have been true of the sculptures on the Shaiva temples such as the Vishvanath and Kandariya Mahadeva, but fails to explain their presence on Vaishnava temples like the Lakshman, or on Jain temples such as Parsvanath.

These celestial beauties are mere "embodied intellect", fragments of divine inspiration and "built up by movement only". Whatever the form — *Surasundari, Nayika, Shalbhanjika* — the divine grace and power of their form emanates from *Shakti* here making itself manifest to man.

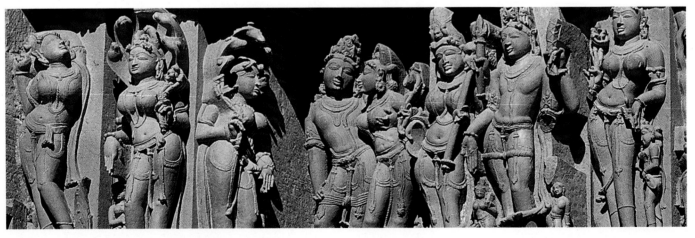

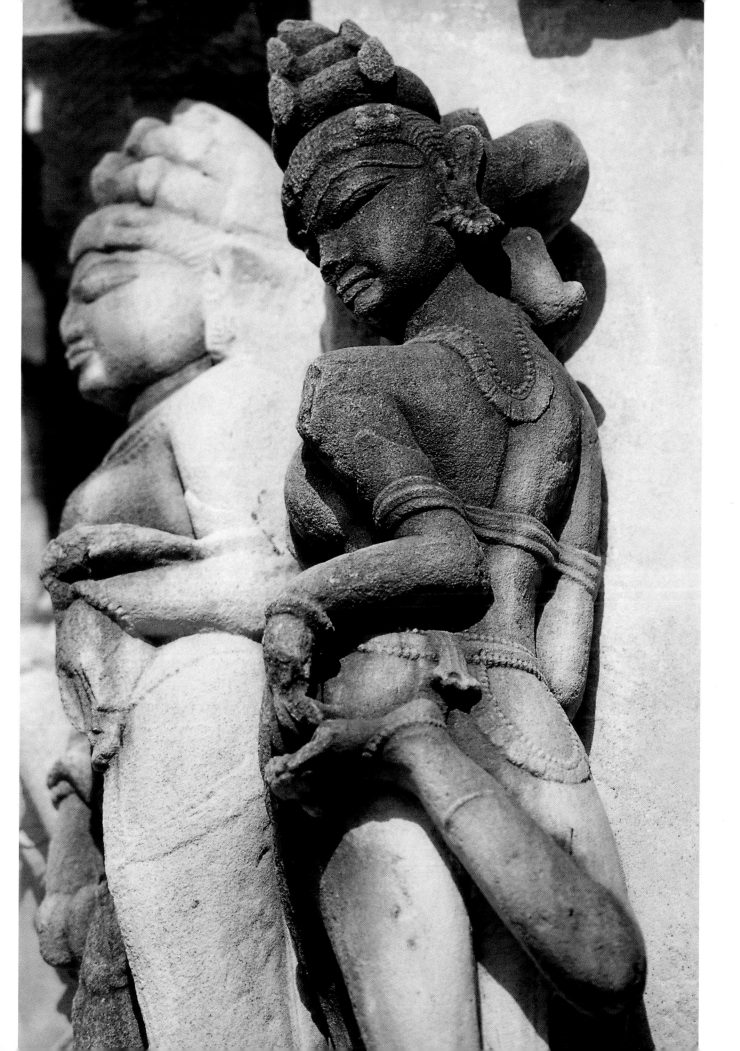

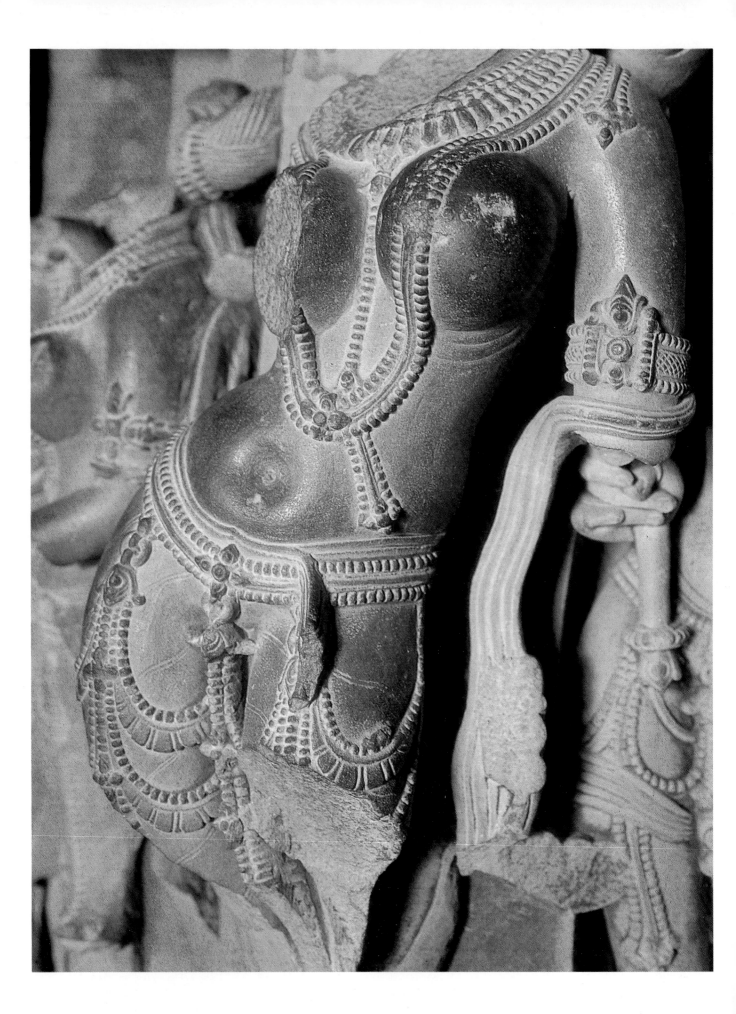

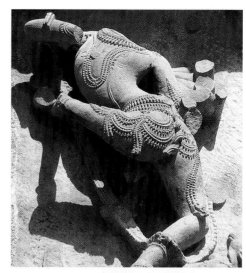

The convex form in Indian sculpture has drawn the attention of the noted art critic, Philip Rawson. This is true of the whole range of figure sculpture on these Chandella temples. Figures seem to burst forth with the sap of life and breath pulsating with youthful vigour. The costumes — for they do exist — and jewellery accentuate their sensuousness. Diaphanous clothing clings to sinuously tapering limbs. The body looks bare but for engraved patterns of print and ornamentation. Folds of loose garments and dangling jewellery have been avoided lest they divert the eye from the natural splendour of form. Even the criss-crossing of limbs is taboo, for the sculptor hoped to retain the visual continuity of line. The clarity of contours is a major factor contributing to the impact of the figural sculpture. For the same reason, perhaps all concavities have been avoided — the Khajuraho sculptors fascinated by the rhythmic rise and fall of body contours.

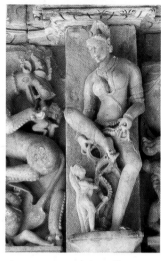

(above): Dancer tying her anklet bells, Parsvanath temple, Eastern Group.
(top): The seventh incarnation of Vishnu as represented at Duladeo temple, Southern Group.
(facing page): Detail of the jewellery worn by a celestial maiden, Devi Jagdamba temple, Western Group.

Punctilious attention has been paid to the coiffed of hair, and the jewellery worn to ornament the headgear. Locks, tresses, buns, coronets, diadems and stringed pearls not only add to the verticality of the composition but also provide a suitable culmination to the erotically taut limbs. Also, "this introduces into the figure sculpture the element of numerical rhythm...drum beat to the melody of the body surfaces". The face, however, holds the key to the mind and reflects the essence of their being. Mostly sculpted in three-quarter profiles, the face reflects the eternal theme of the "form in the becoming". As Stella Kramrisch explains: "The disparity of the one fully visible half of such a face with the other half, which is not meant to be seen, but is there as an artistic fact, this intermediate state of form is an equivalent of the *vyaktavyakta* the manifest-non-manifest, the transition from potentiality to act". The eyes — fish, lotus or almond-shaped — are not meant to cast seductive glances. They are where the outer world meets the inner world.

What the external grandeur of the body directs us to is a matter of inner light, a higher reality which reflects itself through the myriad shapes and forms one sees on the walls of the temple. Ultimately, the observer is left with the feeling of watching manifestations of the divine. Philip Rawson reflects: "The external sculpture...has a two-fold significance. First of all it represents, as it were, the excrescence towards the surface, outwards, into the realm of visible manifestation, of the creative afflatus of the divine, hidden within it. And then, both its figurative and non-figurative decoration represents a kind of summary of the whole world, of all that exists."

Besides gods and goddesses, celestial beauties and erotic couples known as *mithunas*, the friezes on the basement plinth of many temples depict extremely lively scenes from everyday life consisting of domestic activities, teachers and pupils, dancers and musicians. Some narrative reliefs of historical events have also been sculptured with the same observant eye and penchant for detail. In addition to these scenes, there are numerous hunting and battle scenes which depict the activities of soldiers when not actually fighting battles.

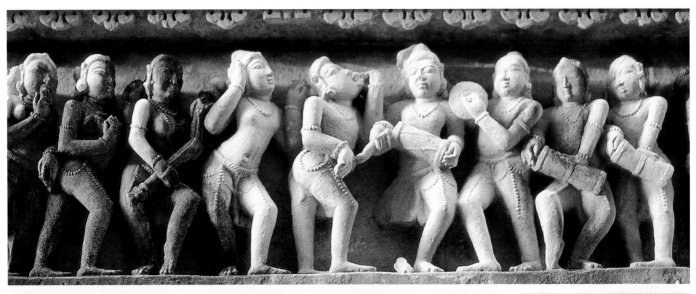

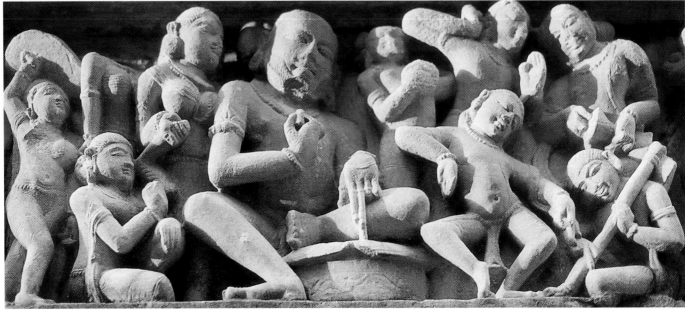

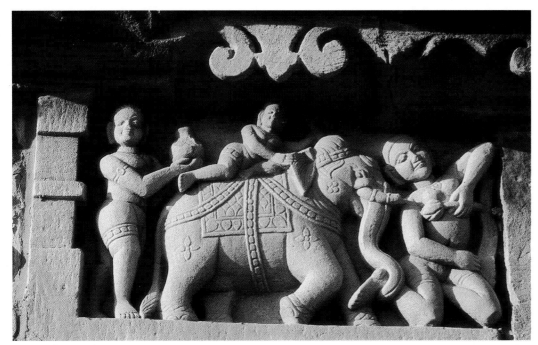

Elephants figure prominently on the sculptured panels. Detailed with great authenticity these beasts of immense power are shown uprooting trees as at the Kandariya Mahadeva temple, or crushing men to death under their monumental weight as at the Lakshman temple. Elephant heads appear as an ornamental band on the plinth, just below the *jangha* at the Lakshman temple, and at the Nandi pavilion. The lion and tiger have interchangeable shapes, appearing as the *sardula*, usually represented with the head of a lion, or sometimes of a man or an elephant. Tigers, lions, boars, rams, birds and elephants combine to create bands of relief on the walls of temples in the recesses between piers. The *sardula* has been most frequently repeated with its mouth open and paw raised to attack, yet, ironically, it protects the man supplicating before its rampant stance. The *sardula* embodies in itself the powers of *Prakriti*, *Shakti* and *Maya*. The 'lion and man' carved in the round as an independent piece of sculpture stands at several prominent places: at the corner of the Kandariya Mahadeva platform, at the porch of the Mahadeva shrine, in a corner of the Devi Jagdamba temple platform, near the Lakshman temple. According to Stella Kramrisch, this sculpture alone sums up "the qualities by which medieval Indian sculpture is conspicuous. It is neither baroque nor is it romantic; it has nothing to do with idealism but builds with symbol elements of forms the concrete reality (*Murti*) of the work of art." The sculpture itself is probably derived from the legendary tales of the founder of the Chandella dynasty's capability of fighting bare-handed with lions.

Two other pieces of magnificent animal sculptures are the Varaha and the Nandi, the former an incarnation of Vishnu and the latter as Shiva's vehicle and guardian of his master's shrine. Both monolithic sculptures are splendid works of art. Other than that, animals have been used as decorative emblems on friezes, while Keechak, the dwarf wrestler, and Kirtimukha, the evil demon, are constants atop columns and pillars, and on panels. The monkey appears as a playful companion to the *Nayikas* and *Surasundaris*, while the parrot usually accompanies the rare woman-and-child sculptures. On the other hand, flowers, trees and shrubs are almost non-existent — perhaps unable to compete with the unfolding human drama on the walls.

(above): The elephant isn't used merely as an embellishment since it played an important part in the economy of the region, not only for purposes of war, but in everyday work.
(facing page): Lively scenes from everyday life lend vitality to the temple walls. The depiction of musicians being tutored in the musical notes (top panel) and in performance before a chieftain (bottom panel) are indicative of the importance of dance and music to the Chandellas. These friezes are from the Lakshmana temple, Western Group.

51

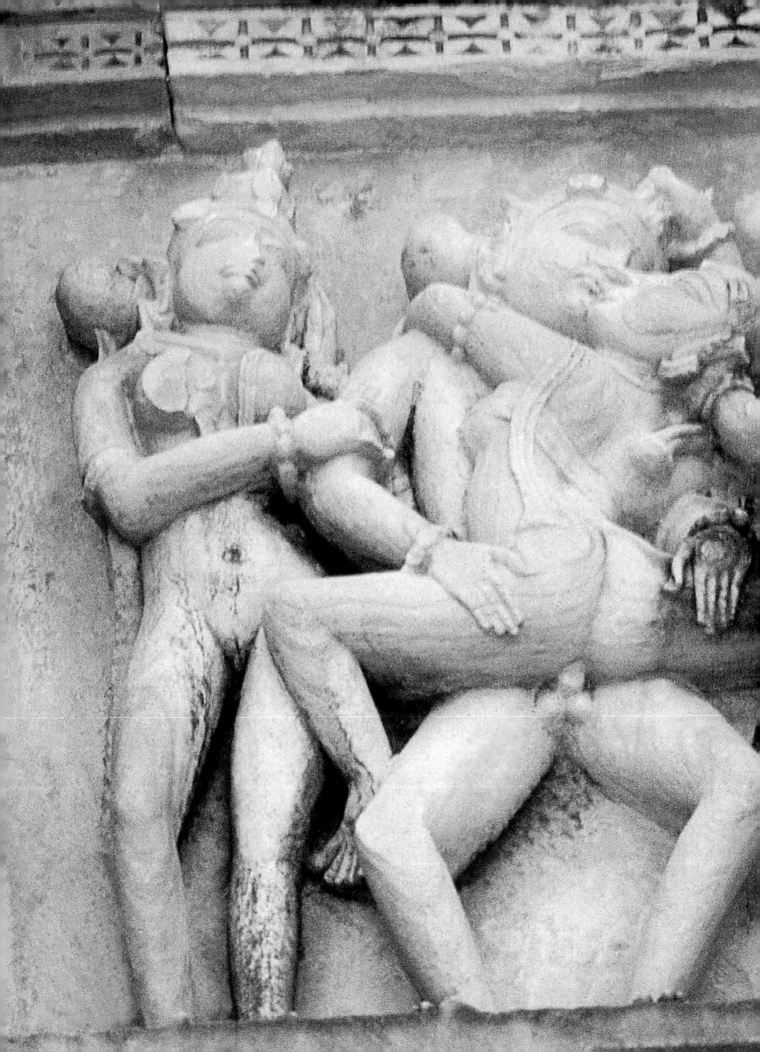

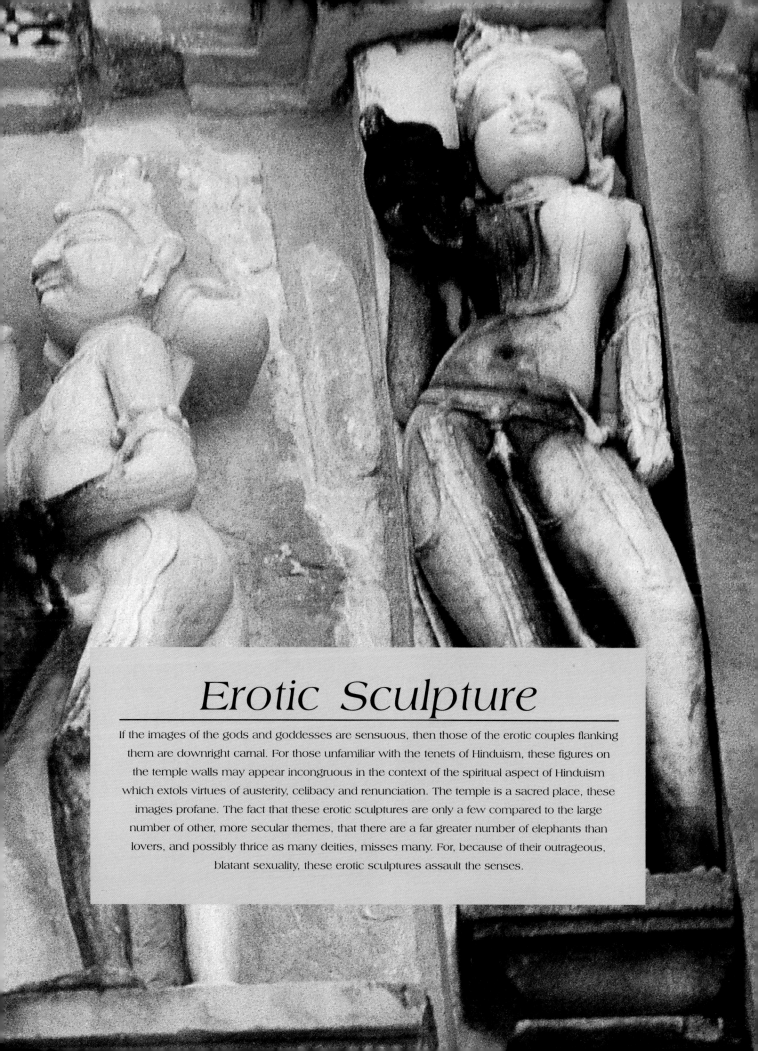

Erotic Sculpture

If the images of the gods and goddesses are sensuous, then those of the erotic couples flanking them are downright carnal. For those unfamiliar with the tenets of Hinduism, these figures on the temple walls may appear incongruous in the context of the spiritual aspect of Hinduism which extols virtues of austerity, celibacy and renunciation. The temple is a sacred place, these images profane. The fact that these erotic sculptures are only a few compared to the large number of other, more secular themes, that there are a far greater number of elephants than lovers, and possibly thrice as many deities, misses many. For, because of their outrageous, blatant sexuality, these erotic sculptures assault the senses.

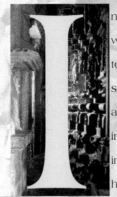

In fact, the initial Western reaction to Khajuraho is a continuation of the disgust with which Capt. T. S. Burt reported his discovery of these temples in 1838. "Hindu temples, are most beautifully and exquisitely carved as to workmanship, but the sculptor had at times allowed his subject to grow a little warmer than there was absolute necessity for his doing; indeed some of the sculptures here were extremely indecent and offensive." Later, Gen. Cunningham also certified them as "highly indecent and most of them disgustingly obscene". This set the trend for a certain highbrow attitude towards Khajuraho's sculpture.

E.B. Havell challenged this view: "No European can understand or appreciate Indian art who does not divest himself of his Western preconceptions, endeavour to understand Indian thought and place himself at the Indian point of view." It requires a more knowledgeable view of Hindu traditions and mythology, and the eschewing of unnecessary comparisons with the Classical art of the West to explore the sensuality of Khajuraho's sculptures, the aesthetics of which had its roots in ancient Indian cultural traditions.

The decoration of religious structures with sexual motifs has been a constant factor in the development of art and architecture, a pan-Indian cultural feature which drew its strength from belief in sexual magic and fertility rites. For the multiplication and revitalisation of life as well as for the aversion of evil, death, misfortune and the promotion of wealth and good luck, sexual motifs exercised a penetrating influence on the social psyche. The concept of the Mother Goddess and fertility cults have been part of an ancient tradition long before we discovered their lineage by excavations at the Chalcolithic sites of Harappa and the Indus Valley Civilisation.

The earliest terracottas evidence the prevalence of fertility cults in the phallic and ring stones. The Harappan seal depicting the male ithyphallic horned god with animal figures is perhaps the earliest image of Shiva as *Pasupati*, Lord of the Animals. Sri, the goddess of opulence, has always been depicted ritualistically exposing her pudenda despite the heavy jewellery girdling her waist. Later, with the secularisation of art, the depiction of *mithuna* couples became an accepted part of temple ornamentation for its auspicious associations. The Buddhist cave at Nasik uses these *mithuna* motifs. The sixth century temples at Aihole and Badami displayed *mithunas* prominently. Places of worship, and hermitages, found nothing paradoxical about their use on *chaitya* doorways and temples.

The rise of Tantrism from the fifth century onwards however, introduced a new factor which revolutionised the nature of sculptural ornamentation on temples. This was an emphasis on the *Yoga*

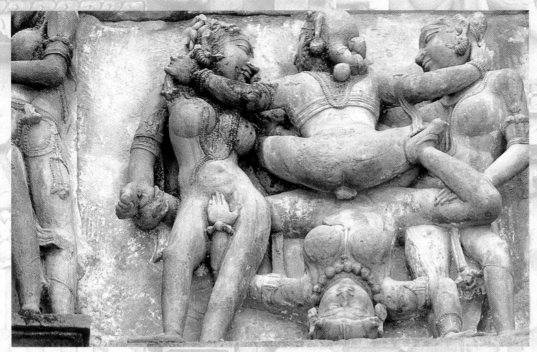

of sexual conjugation as a means of *Moksha* or salvation, using the sensual as the path to the spiritual. The ultimate aim of Tantric *Yogic* regimen was the attainment of spiritual bliss through sexual exercise and retention of semen. The real Tantric *sadhana* aimed at the stabilisation of the three jewels of thought, breath and semen through coitus. Coitus (*maithuna*) was not an act of mere carnal pleasure but an act of liberation for the soul — the union of *Shakti* with *Purusa* in the final state of non-duality.

In its most mature, advanced form, *maithuna* is the union of *Prakriti* and Purusa, twin aspects of the divine self, ever striving to regain primeval unity. The Chandellas had matter-of-factly accepted the male as a symbol of eternity and the female as temporal. It is not surprising that many Indian traditions, particularly the Tantric, see in "human sexual love an essential paradigm and prefiguring of divine union".

For lesser mortals, the Tantric practices offered sex sanctioned by religion. Deviations and degradation followed. The initiation of low-caste women and also the practices of the Vamachara group of Tantrism flaunting their discard of sexual purity and other restrictions; a bland belief in just any man as representative of Shiva and woman as *Shakti*; and using married women for furthering personal perfection of rites.

Directly affecting faith in Tantrism was the concept of *Shakti*, the Supreme Goddess in her numerous forms. Their male counterparts were regarded as inactive and transcendent by themselves for the male gods acted through their *Shaktis*. The whole universe was a creation of their union and the basis of the *advait* (single entity). *Shakti* was the fierce female power, source of universal energy and activity. At the Chausath *Yogini* temple, Kali was the chief goddess, evidence of the popularity of *Shakti* cult, prior to the building of Khajuraho temples by Chandella rulers.

Bundelkhand, or Jejakabhukti, the land of the Chandellas, formed part of a tribal belt under the influence of archaic fertility cults. Agricultural festivals were celebrated and ritualistic copulation in the field marked auspicious occasions such as the sowing of the seeds. The use of erotic language and

(above): This erotic frieze from the Vishvanath temple depicts the carnal as the essential path Hindus had to follow in their quest for the sublime.
(preceding page): The use of sexual motifs in art and architecture draws its inspiration from fertility rites, and has been generously portrayed in Khajuraho. The art is in no way offensive to the tenets of Hinduism.

gestures, and the exposure of male and female genitalia, formed part of the celebrations. The Duladeo temple at Khajuraho celebrates the ancient myth of the young bridegroom married and then killed in these ritualistic festivities. The tribal community knew few inhibitions in sexual matters.

To the visitor from the West, the *ShivaLinga* appears an outrageous symbol of sexuality but is, in fact, "more sacred than any anthropomorphic image". For more than two thousand years the *Linga* has been enshrined in every Shiva temple, symbol of Shiva's tremendous *Yogic* power and sexuality. Shiva, as the great ascetic, has commanded the greatest respect among his devotees. The Gudimallam ShivaLinga (in south India) is the earliest example of a naturalistically sculptured *Linga* dating between the 2nd and 1st centuries BC. The *Linga* shape was subsequently refined to its present form as a divine shaft of light which on its first manifestation had turned the entire cosmos into a ball of fire. The *Linga* is not Shiva, the Great God, but it is through the form of the *Linga* that Shiva manifests himself.

The ithyphallic shape has immense symbolic significance as it epitomises the culmination of a strenuous *Yogic* discipline. It stands for seminal retention, absolute self control and the renunciation of carnal desires. It reveals for us Shiva, the great *Yogi*, "whose seed is drawn up, whose *Linga* is raised". The *Linga* is symbolic of creation, liberation and annihilation, "the most direct parallel for the numinous power of the divine", promising transcendental bliss to the *Yogi*. The Tantric concept of transmutation of sexual power into mental power and of channelling the procreative into creative faculty derives immeasurable support from the force imminent in the *Linga*.

When Shiva's *Linga* fell off in the forest and a great fire raged all around the gods propitiated him to take it back. But only Parvati could hold the divine phallus in her *yoni*. She agreed to hold Shiva's phallus in her *yoni*, the sacred female sex organ which became a cult object and, together with the *Linga*, came to be installed in Shiva shrines. Its elongated spout-like shape also allowed the water and milk poured on the sacred shaft to flow out. But the urdhvaLinga placed within the *yoni* does not penetrate it; instead, it rises out of it. It is also believed that the great sage Bhrigu called on Shiva when the Lord was in the deep embrace of Parvati. Pained at being neglected by Shiva, Bhrigu cursed him in his lust and said henceforth he would be worshipped in the shape of the *Linga* and *yoni*.

Theological speculations of the *Shaivas* and *Shaktas*, their common belief in the creative female energy and power of *Yoga*, and the ultimate identification with the supreme god helped Tantrism gain favour among the people, whether commoners, royals or feudatories. Many sexual rituals of the Tantrics and *Yogic* exercises were devised to create the divine bliss crystallised in the image of the *ShivaLinga*.

Tantrism also drew towards it several unscrupulous hedonists who cared little for *Yoga* or austerities. The feudal lords and the *Devadasi* system contributed to the general decline in morals. Even Jain and Buddhist monks fell prey to this licentiousness. The Khajuraho sculptures depict many such monks (with beards) enjoying themselves with women. Prabodhachandrodayam, a contemporary drama in Sanskrit, refers to the decadence in morals among the clergy. The orgiastic scenes amply establish that sex was no longer confined to the strict privacy of a room but conducted openly with the assistance of male and female attendants. Perversions led to the inclusion of animals in the wild pursuit of

(facing page): While the erotic friezes draw inference to Khajuraho being at the centre of tantric cults who drew on sexual energy, it is possible the representation may have simply been mundane: Hindu temples often use erotic elements to ward off the 'evil eye', though these are usually hidden from view and not thrust prominently into it, as in the case of Khajuraho.

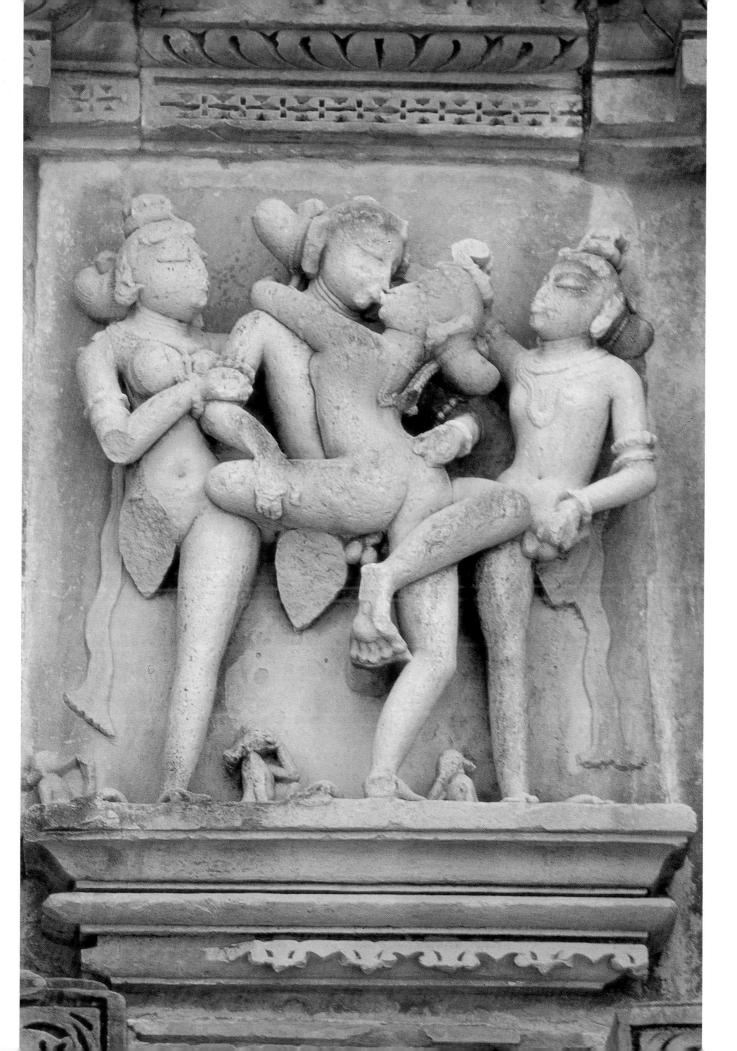

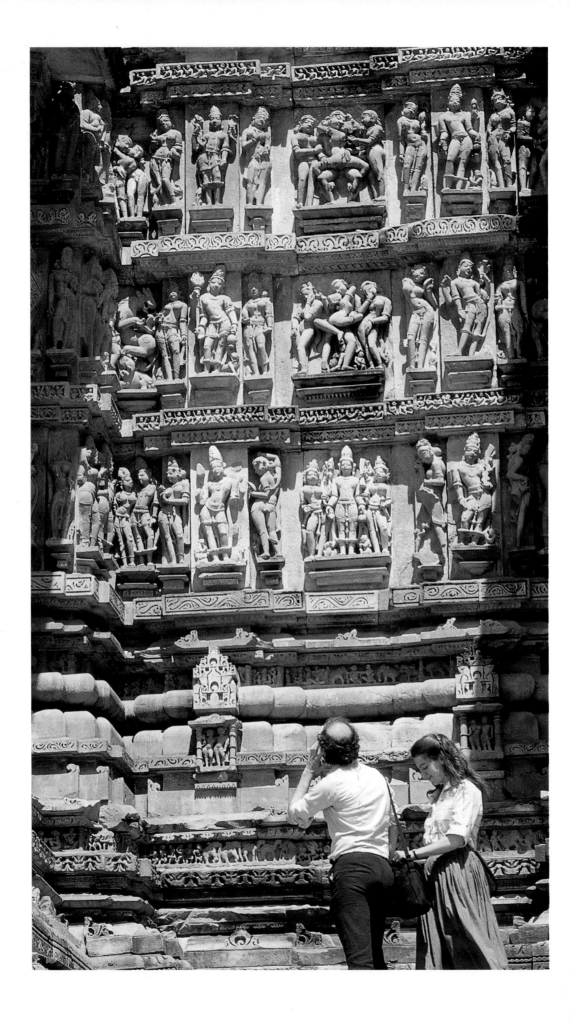

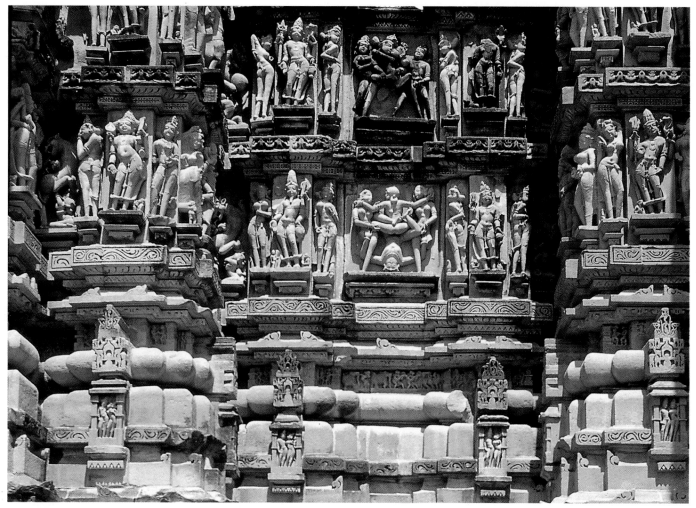

pleasure. Ibn Battuta in 1325 had seen yellow skinned *Yogis* preparing aphrodisiacs and the long panel on the plinth of the Lakshman temple vividly portrays sexual practices in the Chandella capital.

Theories have also been suggested that the erotic sculpturing was a ploy to attract people back to the temples for Buddhism had made major inroads as a religion, and the Hindu priests were concerned by the dwindling interest in Hinduism. Once the people flocked to the temples, the priests were sure the spirituality of the atmosphere and the sermons would retain their interest. It has also been suggested that the erotic chapters sculpted on the walls may have been a means of ensuring a healthy, wedded life for young men who had spent the early years of their life in ashrams, away from their families — a common practise in Hindu society. The carnal pleasures, it was understood, needed to be accepted by them as one of the features of domestic life which would lead, over time, to a higher, more spiritual plane.

Perhaps the best defense for Khajuraho's sensuous art comes from Charles Fabri: "This is great art; it is passionate; it is fervent; it is burning with the fever of inspiration. The cold calculation that makes pornography is totally absent. This is an impassioned appeal by the artist to you to share his rapture, his ravishment in the beauty of love; an ecstatic exclamation about a subject on which he feels deeply — and it is difficult if not impossible not to be infected by such an ecstasy."

Or, perhaps, the best way to admire the erotic sculpture at Khajuraho is to see it as "a manifestation of the sophistication, not without a certain playfulness", as J.C. Harle suggests.

(above): The sculptural bands from Kandariya Mahadev temple best represent Charles Fabri's view of them as "an impassioned appeal by the artist...to share his rapture, his ravishment in the beauty of love".

(facing page): Mithuna or erotic couples usually form the central band of the sculptures, and these are flanked by a wealth of other sculptures. It is therefore inappropriate to view them in isolation, but enjoy them for "a certain playfulness".

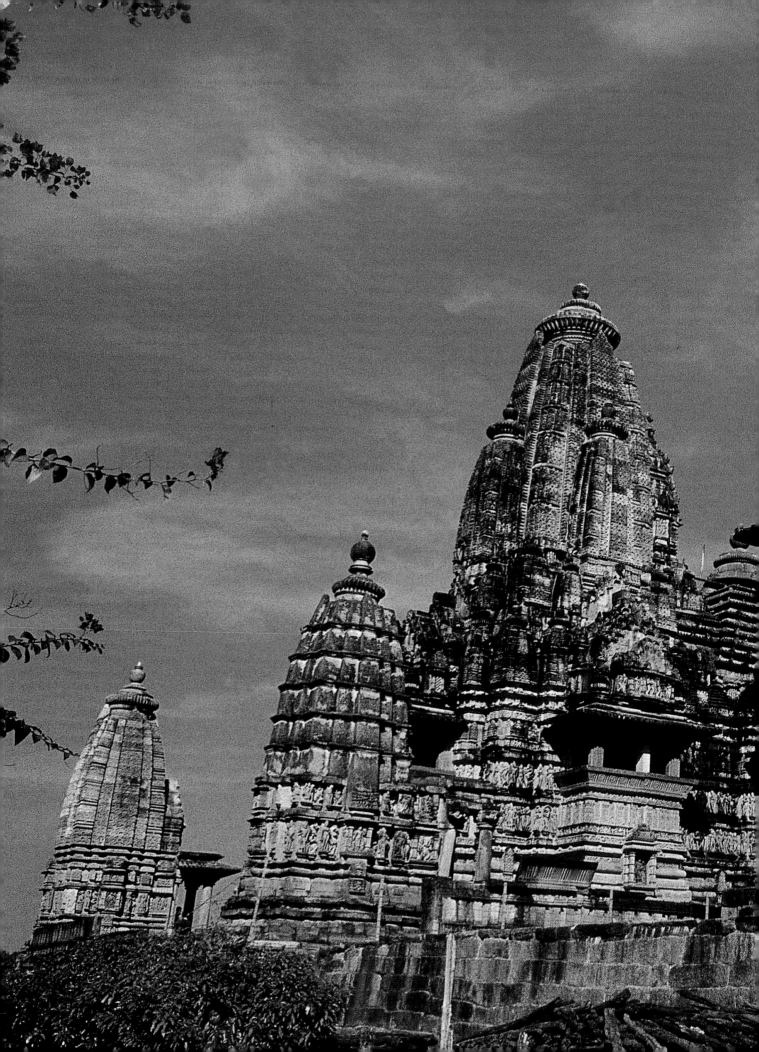

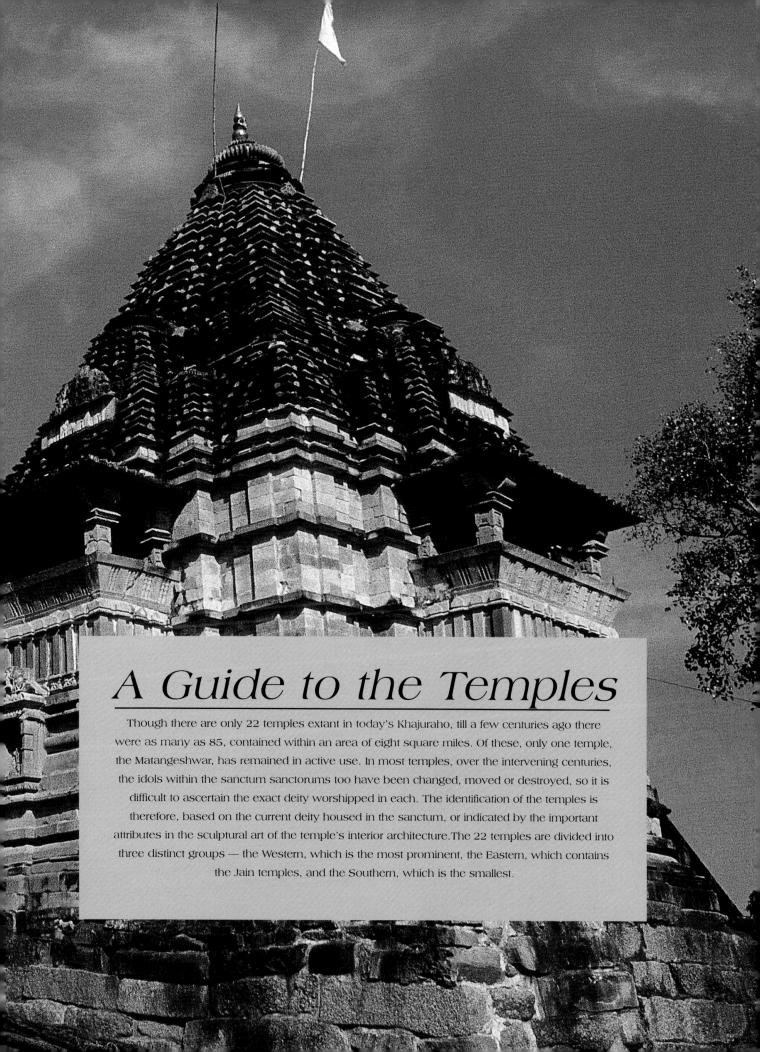

A Guide to the Temples

Though there are only 22 temples extant in today's Khajuraho, till a few centuries ago there were as many as 85, contained within an area of eight square miles. Of these, only one temple, the Matangeshwar, has remained in active use. In most temples, over the intervening centuries, the idols within the sanctum sanctorums too have been changed, moved or destroyed, so it is difficult to ascertain the exact deity worshipped in each. The identification of the temples is therefore, based on the current deity housed in the sanctum, or indicated by the important attributes in the sculptural art of the temple's interior architecture. The 22 temples are divided into three distinct groups — the Western, which is the most prominent, the Eastern, which contains the Jain temples, and the Southern, which is the smallest.

Major Temples of Khajuraho

Name	Year consecrated (c.)	Principal deity	Group
Chausath *Yogini*	850	64 *Yogini*s depicting different aspects of *Shakti*	Western
Lalguan Mahadeva	900	Shiva (no image)	Western
Matangeshwar	900-925	Shiva*Linga*	Western
Varaha	900-925	Vishnu's boar incarnation	Western
Brahma	925	Shiva (earlier Vishnu)	Eastern
Lakshman	954	Vishnu	Western
Parsvanath	954	Parsvanath/Jain (earlier Adinath, even earlier Hindu)	Eastern
Ghantai	end 10th century	Jain	Eastern
Parvati	950-1000	Parvati	Western
Chitragupta	1000	Surya	Western
Devi Jagdamba	1000	Parvati (earlier Vishnu)	Western
Nandi	1002	Nandi	Western
Vishvanath	1002	Shiva*Linga*	Western
Kandariya Mahadeva	1025	Shiva*Linga*	Western
Shantinath	1028	Adinath/Jain	Eastern
Vamana	1050-75	Vishnu in dwarf form	Eastern
Javari	1075-1100	Vishnu	Eastern
Adinath	11th century	Modern image of Adinath	Eastern
Chaturbhuj	1100	Shiva	Southern
Duladeo	1100-1125	Shiva (earlier Kartikeya)	Southern

(right): The remarkable achievement of the Khajuraho sculptor was the plasticity he was able to bring to his work, combining the fantastic with the realistic.

(preceding page): A view of Matangeshwara temple in the foreground where worship at the sanctum still takes place. In the background is the Lakshmana temple, part of the Western Group, and the most perfect representation of the panchanan (five shrines) style.

Chausath Yogini

Built of coarse granite, this is the oldest extant temple in Khajuraho and has 64 cells belonging to Goddess Kali and her 64 supporting *Shaktis*. The cells have small, curvilinear *shikharas*. Only three images have survived — those of *Brahmani, Maheshwari* and *Mahisasuramardini*. The squat, massive form of the images has little ornamentation but is replete with an elemental energy and ruggedness characteristic of the earliest sculptures of Khajuraho. Built on an oblong plan on a 15 ft-high platform, the Chausath *Yogini* temple has an unusual rectangular layout whereas most contemporary *Yogini* temples are circular and hypaethral. Standing in the fields, the Chausath *Yogini* is a fascinating ruin.

Lalguan Mahadeva

Close to the Chausath *Yogini* stands the small Lalguan Mahadeva temple dedicated to Shiva. Built on a granite platform, the temple faces west and a small Nandi (Shiva's mount, the bull) has been placed in front of the sanctum. The portico has disappeared. The Lalguan belongs to the transitional phase when sandstone was used along with granite.

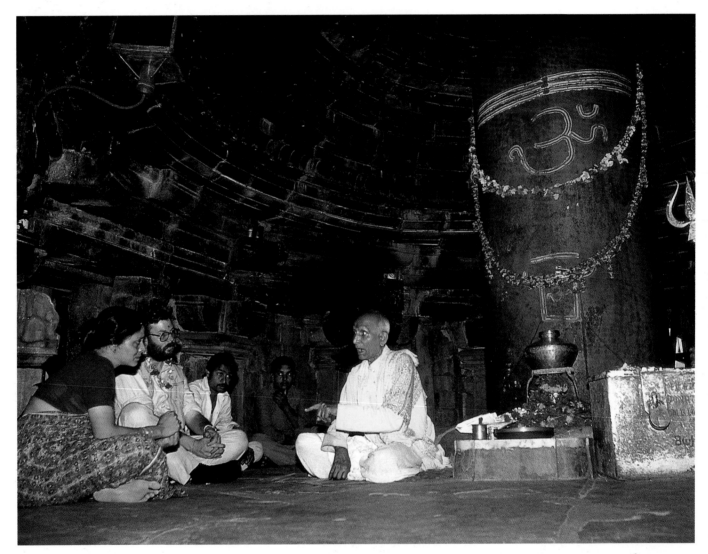

Matangeshwara

(above and facing page): At Matangeshwara temple, the sanctum is still open to the faithful, and images are often submerged in petals and vermilion. The sanctum houses one of the largest Shiva lingas in the country.

Standing on the northern bank of the Shivsagar pond, and near the Lakshman temple, the sandstone-built Matangeshwara contains one of the largest *ShivaLingas* to be found in India. 8 ft., 4 in. in height, on a large *gauripatta* with a diameter of 20 ft., 4 in. occupying the entire floor area in the main hall. The Matangeshwara is the only temple where devotees still flock to worship the Shiva*Linga* as they have done for centuries. It is possible that this temple was built as a memorial to Dhanga who, it is chronicled, lived for over a hundred years.

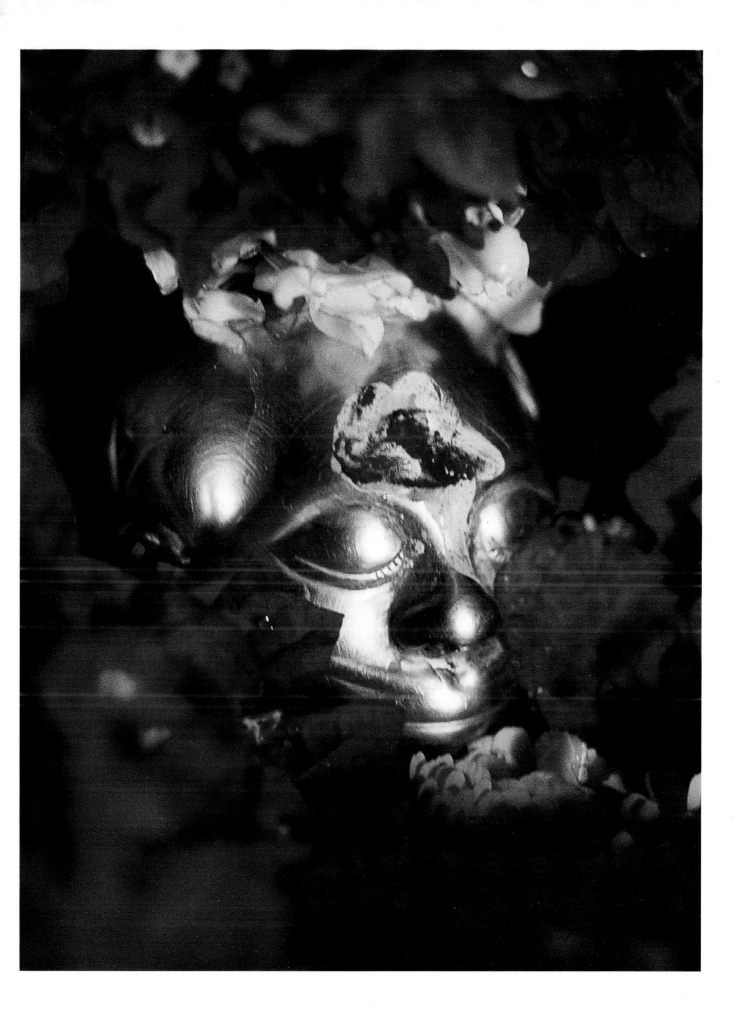

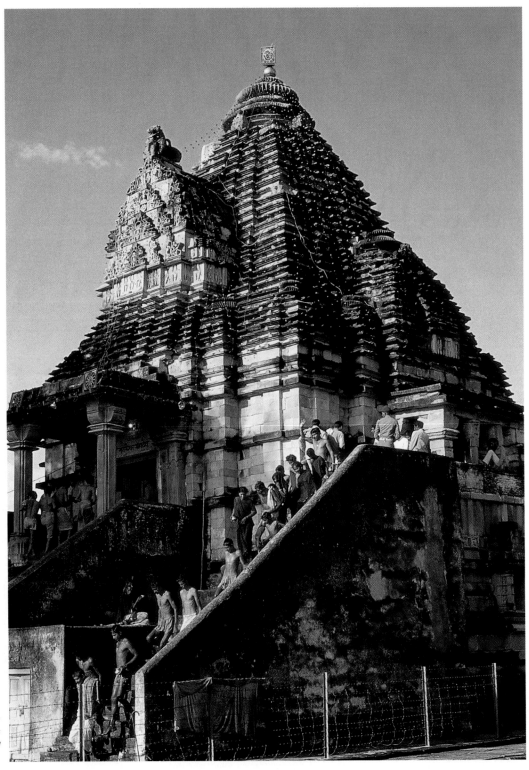

(right): Visitors use a steep flight of stairs to traverse the platform on which the Matangeshwara temple is located. On Shivratri, the entire area is crowded with Shiva worshippers.
(facing page): The boar incarnation of Vishnu as depicted in the Varaha temple consists of a monolithic statue carved with 674 images of gods, goddesses, the planets, snakes and the guardians of the four cardinal points, placed in neat rows.

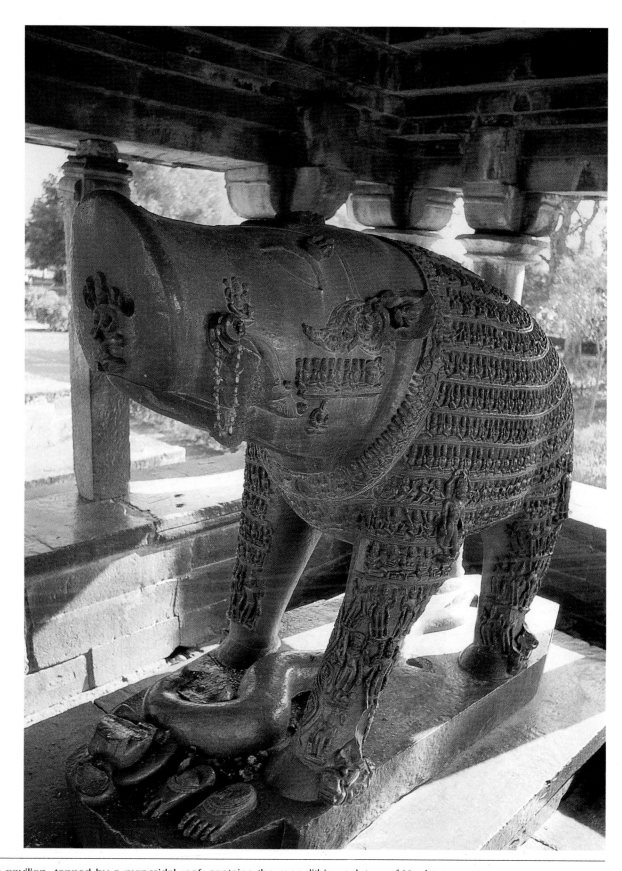

Varaha

The Varaha pavilion, topped by a pyramidal roof, contains the monolithic sculpture of Varaha, Vishnu's incarnation as the boar to rescue earth from the clutches of a demon. The entire body of this 8 ft. 9 in long statue is covered with 674 small images of gods and goddesses in neat rows. This is one of the most exquisitely carved statues in Khajuraho.

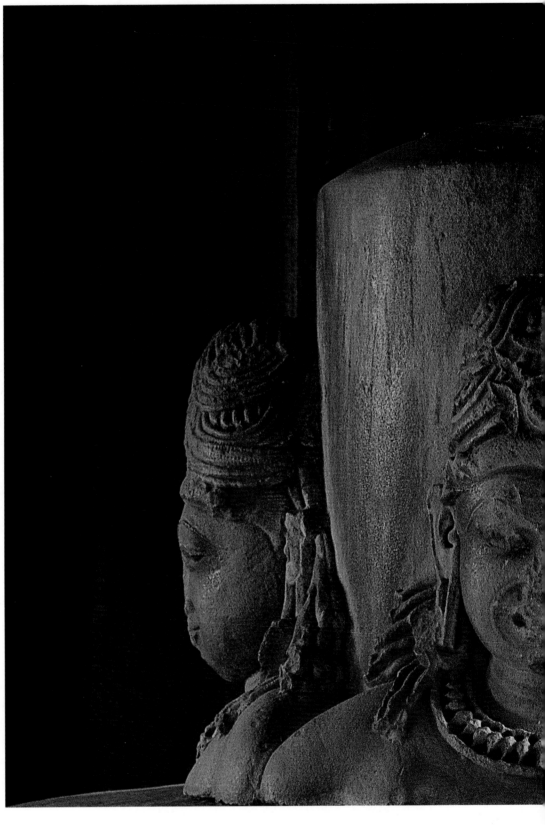

The Brahma temple (facing page)
uses granite and sandstone and
fronts a lake in the Eastern Group.
Within the sanctum is a linga
(right) with images of Shiva carved
in all four cardinal directions.
Among the earliest temples, it is fairly
simple in its execution.

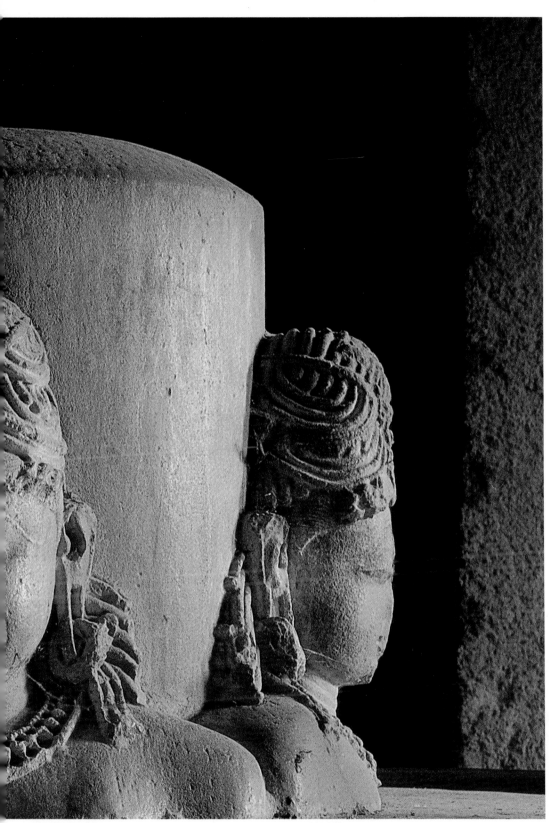

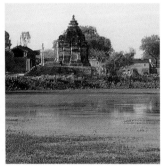

Brahma

Among the oldest temples in Khajuraho, the Brahma temple is made of both granite and sandstone and topped by a pyramidal *shikhara*. Erroneously named after Brahma, the west-facing sanctum contains a four-faced *Linga* making it a Shiva temple. The image of Vishnu appears on the lintel of the sanctum doorway. The lattice window on the back wall is a modern feature.

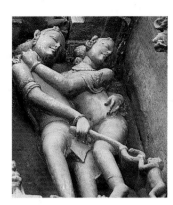

Lakshmana

As the Chandellas grew in power, their temples became increasingly more elaborate in detail and surface ornamentation. Built only 50 years after the Chausath *Yogini*, the Lakshman temple shows remarkable advancement in technique and plan over the rudimentary structures of earlier temples. It is typical of the fully evolved *panchayatana* or five-sect plan. All four of its corner shrines still stand on the high platform with the grand structure in the centre. Built by Yashovarman, the temple is dedicated to Vaikunthnath, a form of Vishnu with three heads, respectively those of the lion, boar and man.

The plinth of the temple structure contains decorative friezes depicting battle and hunting scenes, pageants of soldiers and horses and, on top a band of elephant heads. On the *jangha* portion is a double row of statuary containing splendid images of gods, celestial beauties, erotic couples and *sardulas*, each carved to perfection. The projected balconies create a dramatic balance of solids and voids, light and shade. The various *mandapas* have separate pyramidal roofs, stepped tiers with tile ribbings. The *shikhara* is covered with *chaitya*-window motifs. The chief feature of the *shikhara* is the host of *urushringas* around the *mulamanjari*.

The *ardha mandapa* is decorated with a two-looped *makara-torana* (an architectural embellishment that forms an entrance arch emanating from the mouths of crocodiles) forced open by two gladiators. This particular looped arch is a particularly good piece of sculpture. The graded floors of the *mandapa* lead to the sanctum. The interior pillars are richly covered with sculpture. There are eight figures on each column, and the doorway to the sanctum has 108 figures, symbolic of the 108 techniques of stilling the mind as taught to Shiva and Parvati. The south-east face of the terrace on which the temple stands has a long frieze depicting a scene of sexual orgy and the preparation of aphrodisiacs.

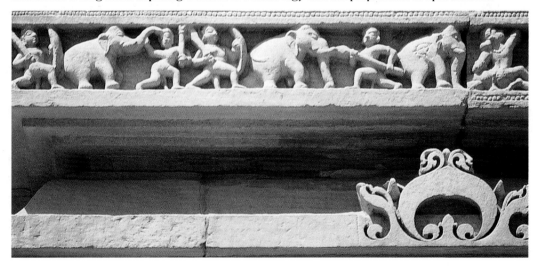

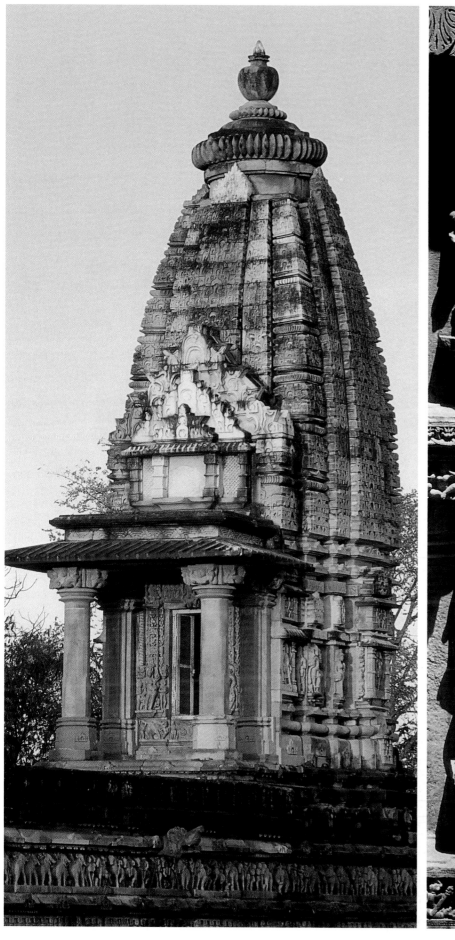
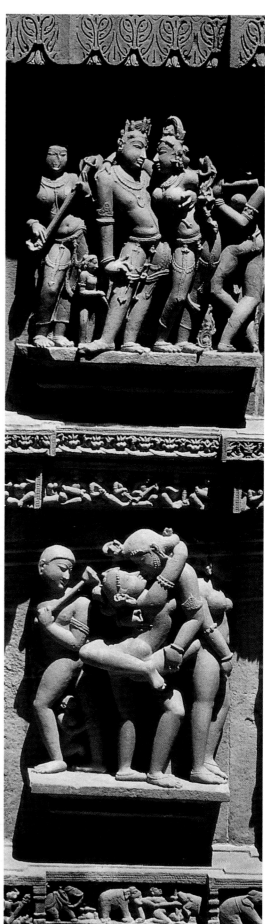

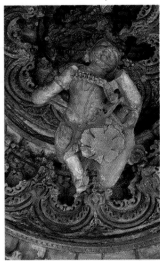

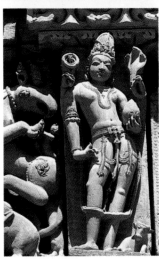

The largest and best preserved of the Eastern Group, the Parsvanath temple (facing page, above) is made of sandstone and is designed like a Hindu temple, even though it is dedicated to a Jain tirthankara. The ceiling at the entrance is exquisitely carved (facing page, below). Its sculptures (this page) consist of some of the finest seen in Khajuraho, and include Hindu and Jain deities, as well as several secular figures of dancers.

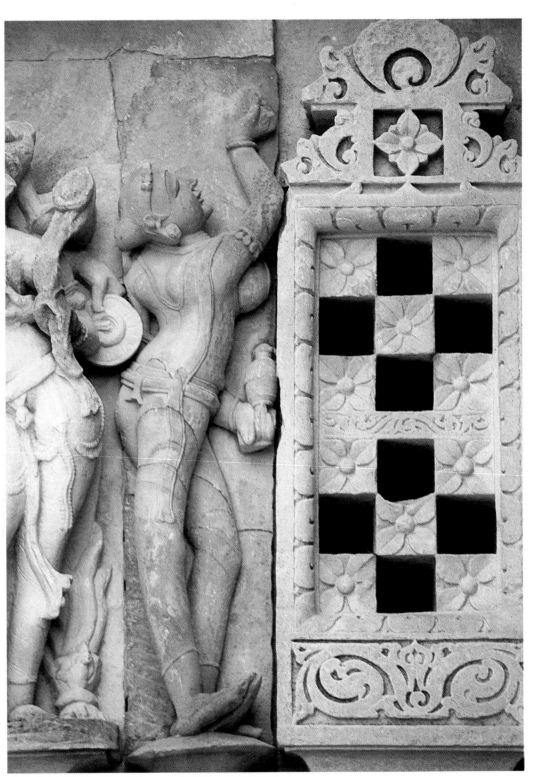

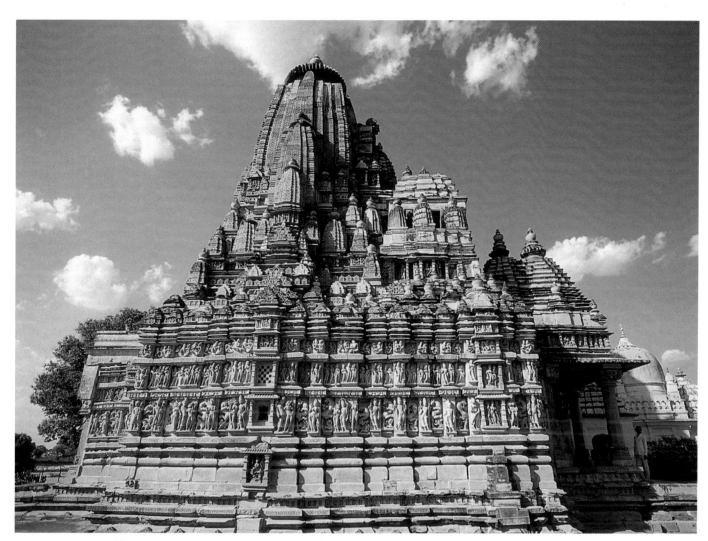

Parsvanath

In construction, a contemporary of the Lakshman, the Parsvanath is the largest of the Jain temples. It contains marvellous sculptures of divine couples and *Surasundaris*. The most exquisite are those of Shiva-Parvati, of a *Nayika* or beautiful woman removing a thorn from her foot, and another applying kohl to her eyes. The temple is smaller than the Kandariya Mahadeva but the bands of sculpture are a visual feast of figures sculpted to perfection. The interior ceilings are ingenious in design and the entrance porch is the most ornate of its kind in Khajuraho. In the absence of the projecting balconied windows the facade looks relatively monotonous. The black marble image of Adinath in the sanctum was placed in 1860. Though repairs on the temple have been carried out the basic structure is original and typical of Chandella architecture.

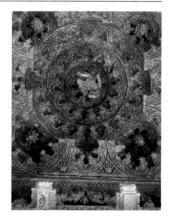

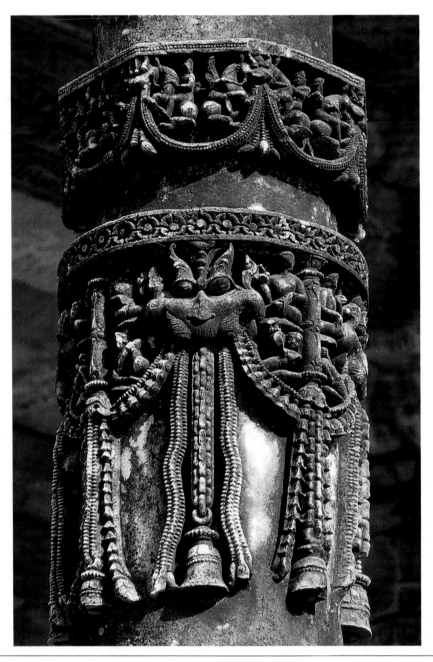

Ghantai

A curious relic of the past, the Ghantai temple is so-named for its skeletons of pillars, each carved with bell and chain motifs. On the door lintel are carved the 16 symbols of the Digamber Jain sect. The pillars resemble the 10th century pillars of temples at the Qutab mosque in Delhi. It remains a mystery whether the temple was left incomplete by its builders or destroyed later by Muslim invaders. A Buddhist image discovered in the debris led to the mistaken belief of the Ghantai being a Buddhist temple, but subsequent excavations unearthed nude Jain images. Further proof that it was a Jain temple came from the 16 dreams of Mahavira's mother carved on the doorway. The Ghantai is among the most fascinating of the temples in Khajuraho and very little is known about it.

Parvati

The Parvati temple has a 4 ft, 4 in high statue of Gauri on her mount, the iguana, in the sanctum. The structure formed part of a bigger edifice which is now completely destroyed.

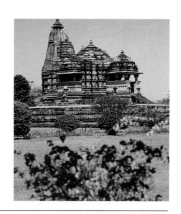

Chitragupta

The Chitragupta temple is noted chiefly for the 4 ft, 10 in high image of Surya, the Sun God, riding his chariot pulled by seven horses representing the seven days of the week. Like the Devi Jagdamba temple, it has no ambulatory. Standing at the northern corner of the compound, the Chitragupta temple contains some exquisite sculpture on the *jangha*. The frieze depicting stone-cutters at work deserves special appreciation. Large scale restoration on the *shikhara* has deprived it of its original grandeur.

(above): Dedicated to Surya, the sun god, the Chitragupta temple has an octagonal ceiling and is in a good state of preservation. Best known for its hunting and dancing scenes, a profusion of floral art (left) also surrounds the girth of the walls.

(facing page): Little is known about the Ghantai temple, but its carved lintel and pillars have a profusion of sculptural details that link it with the Qutab mosque in Delhi.

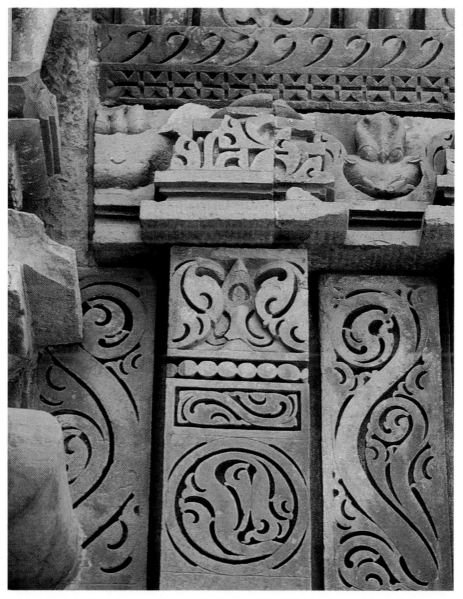

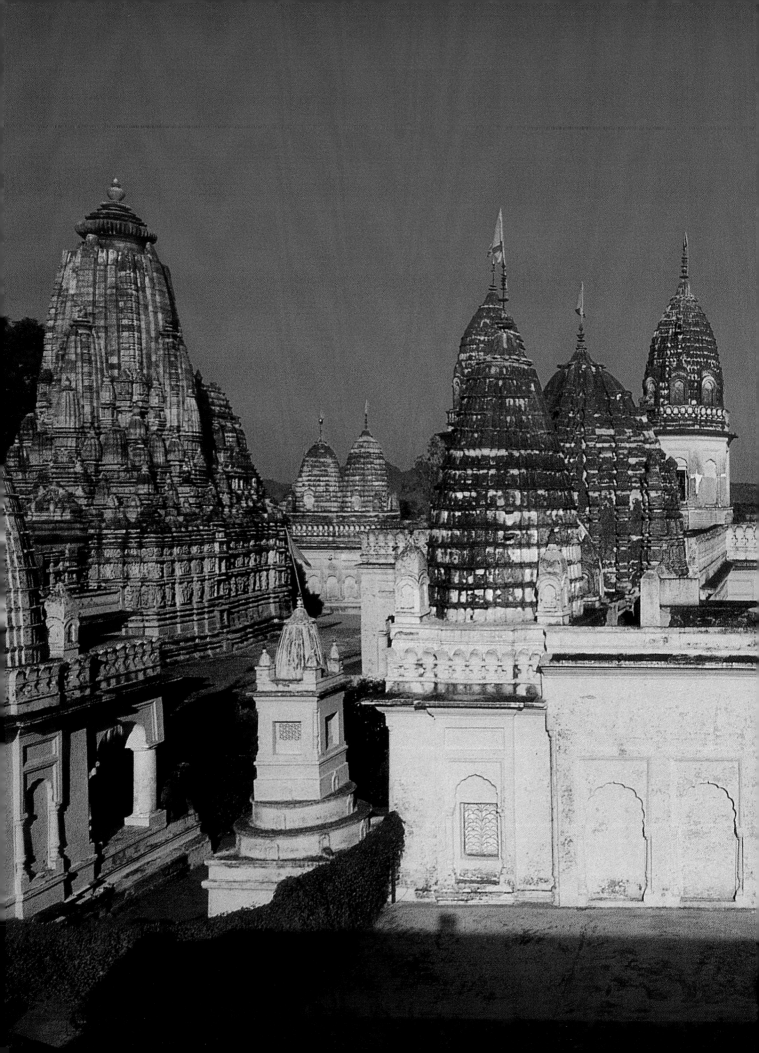

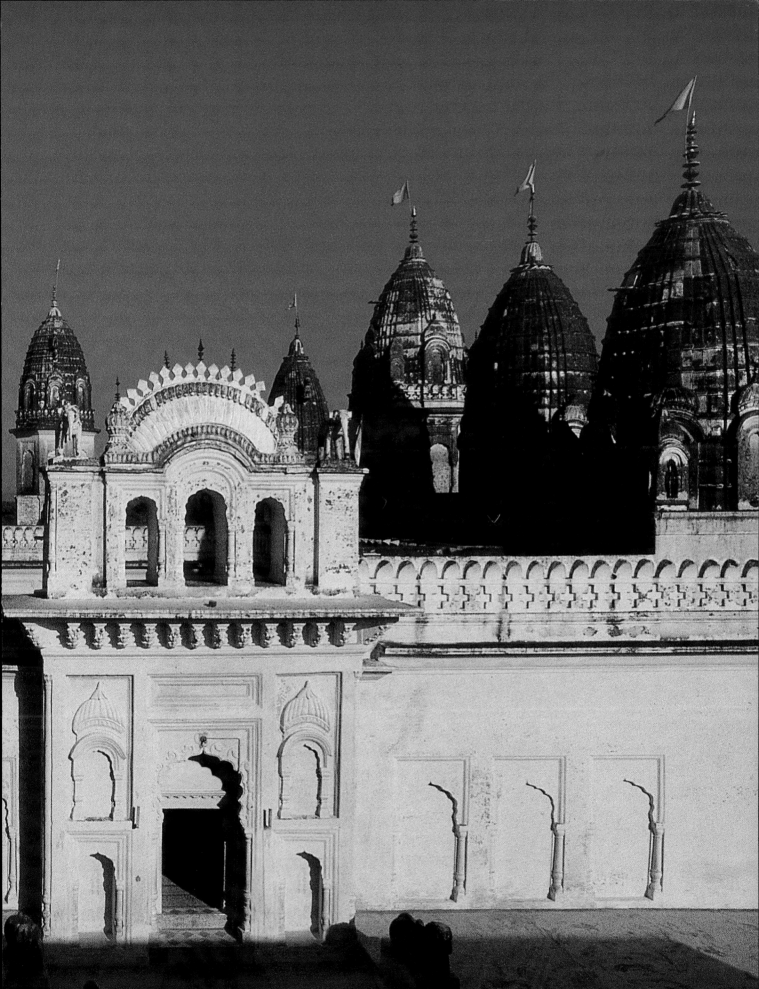

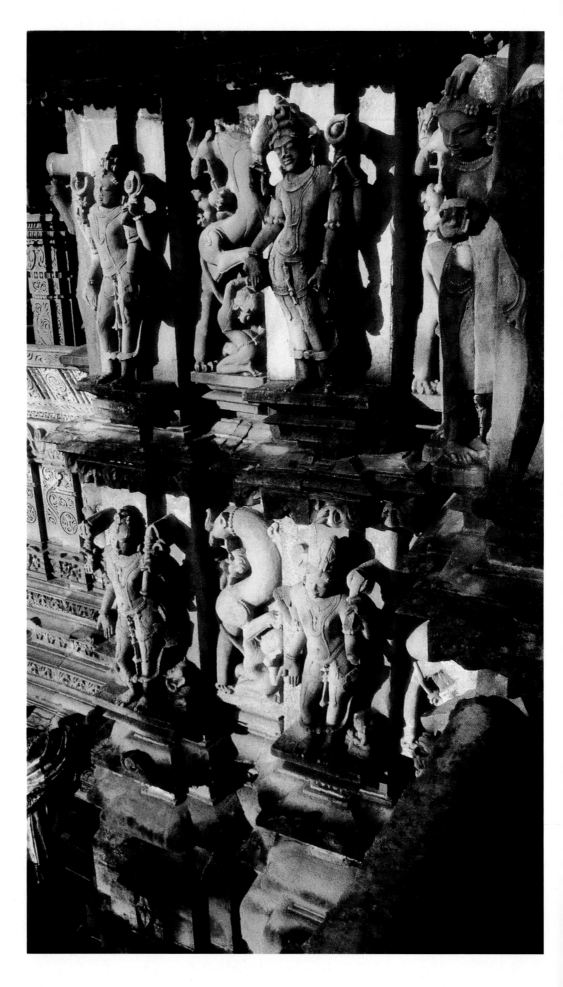

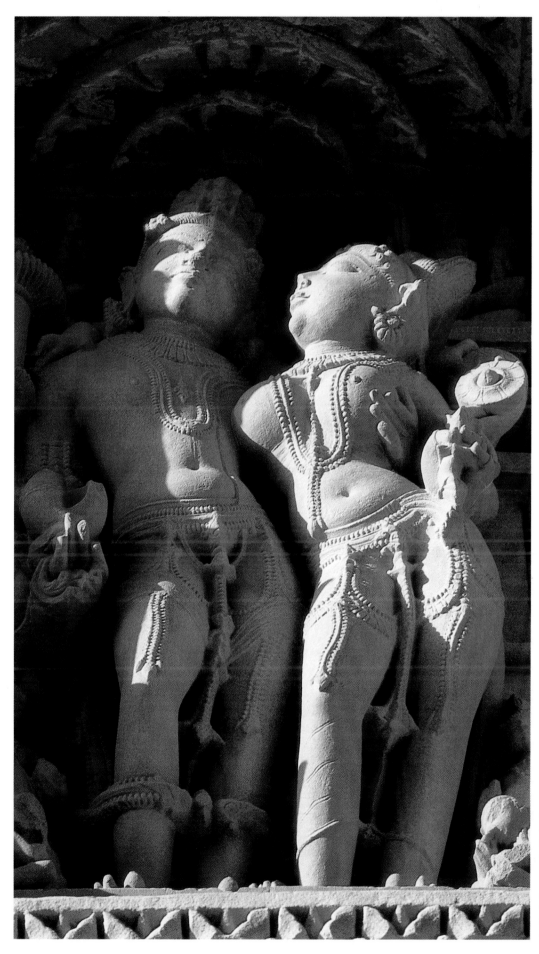

(facing page and left): Three bands of sculptures girdle the Devi Jagdamba temple with a profusion of deities, celestial nymphs, mithunas, figures of women undressing or at their toilette. (preceding page): An overview of the Jain temples of the Eastern Group. A museum at the entrance houses some fine images unearthed from the site.

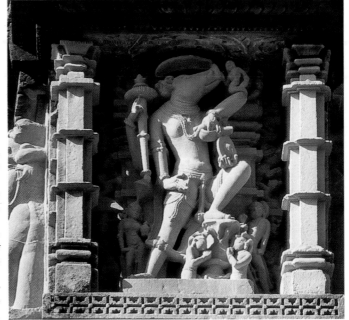

Devi Jagdamba

The small Devi Jagdamba temple is *nirandhara* (one without an ambulatory) housing a black-painted deity, Kali or Lakshmi, in obeisance to the power of *Shakti*, and contains well-proportioned, exquisitely carved erotic sculptures. A three-headed, eight-armed Shiva and a dwarf image of Vishnu are two fascinating pieces of sculpture at the temple which shares its platform with the grand Kandariya Mahadeva.

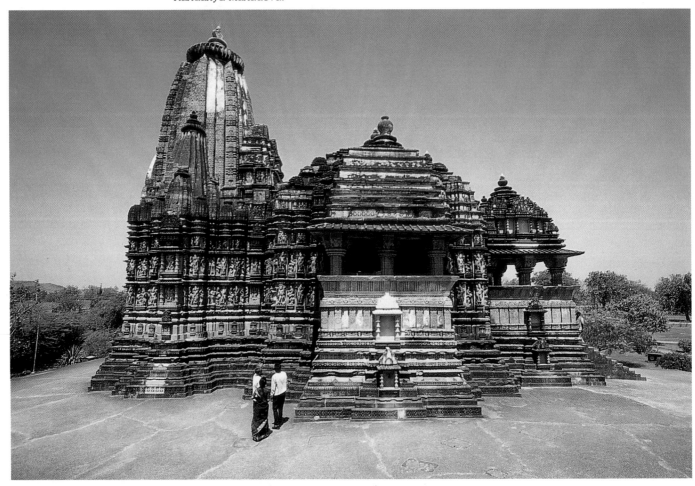

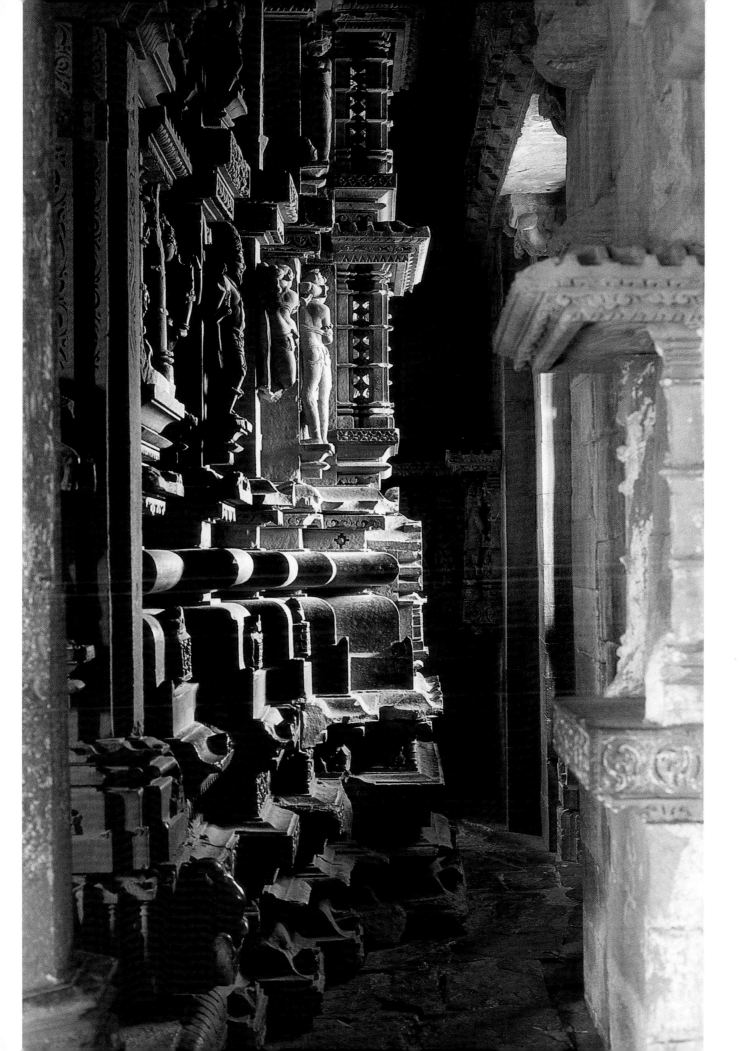

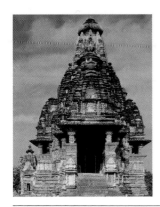

Vishvanath

Dhanga, the most illustrious of the Chandella rulers, completed this Shiva temple and consecrated two *Lingas*, one of emerald and the other of stone. The Vishvanath temple follows the *panchayatana* plan. It is a *sandhara* (with ambulatory around the sanctum) temple with a richly ornamented interior. The triple bands of sculpture on the *jangha* and the mass of *urushringas* around the soaring *shikhara* provide an indication of the perfection these features were to attain in the Kandariya Mahadeva temple.

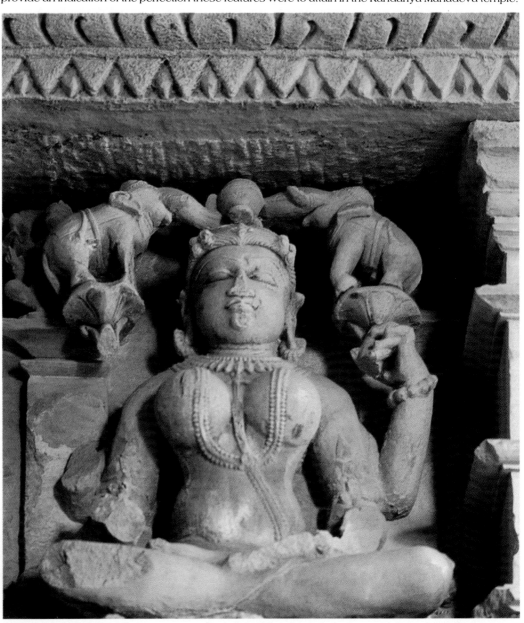

(right): An image of a goddess enshrined inside Vishvanath temple.
(above): Though the Vishvanath temple had four subsidiary shrines, only two are extant. It shares its plinth with a Nandi temple (facing page) which faces the Vishvanath shrine.
(following page): A seated Devi surveys visitors from her niche in the interior of Vishvanath temple.

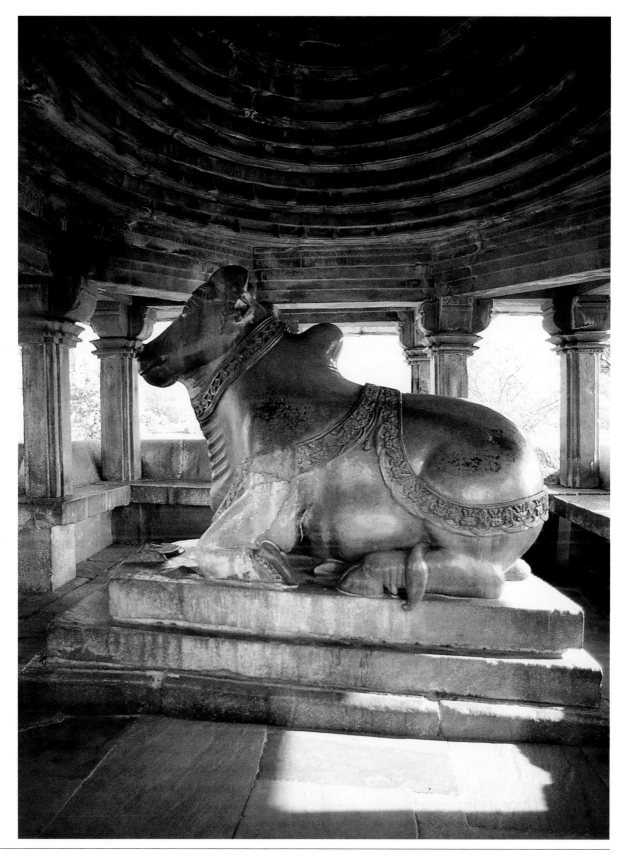

Nandi

In a small, detached pavilion with 12 pillars, facing the sanctum of the Vishvanath temple, sits Nandi, Shiva's mount, representative of the procreative energy of *Shakti* and the counterpoint of the pure spirit, Purusa. This highly polished, monolithic sculpture is absolutely perfect, each limb vibrant with vitality. The pavilion has a pyramidal roof of receding tiers and a circular ceiling.

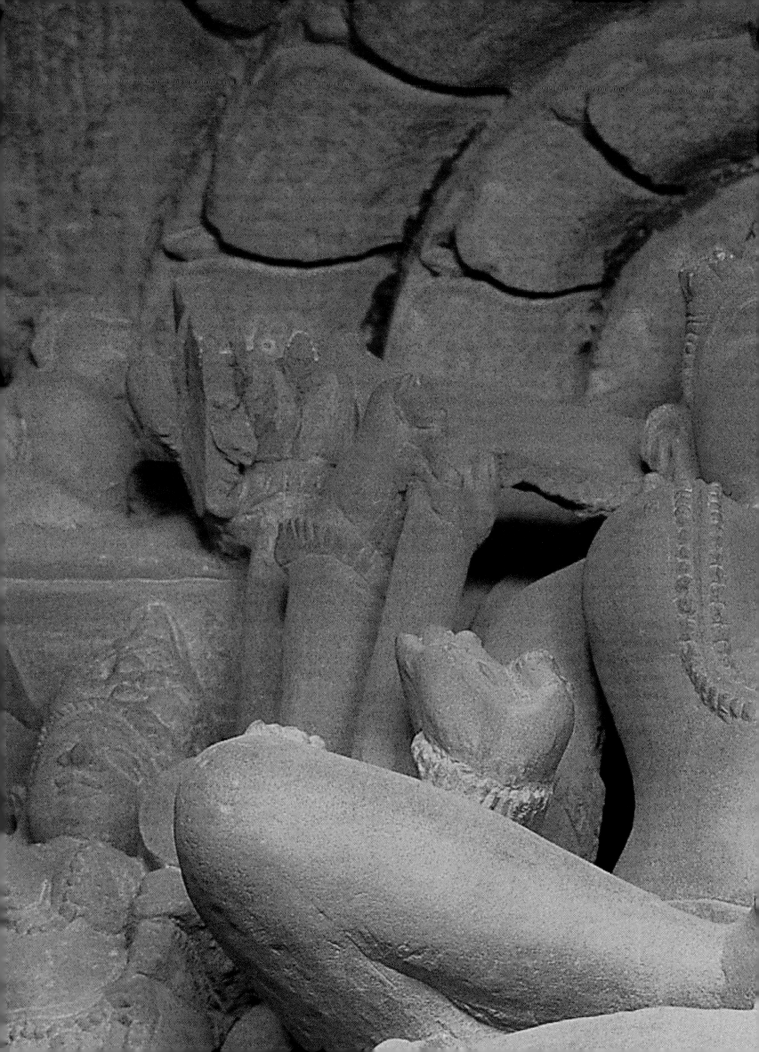

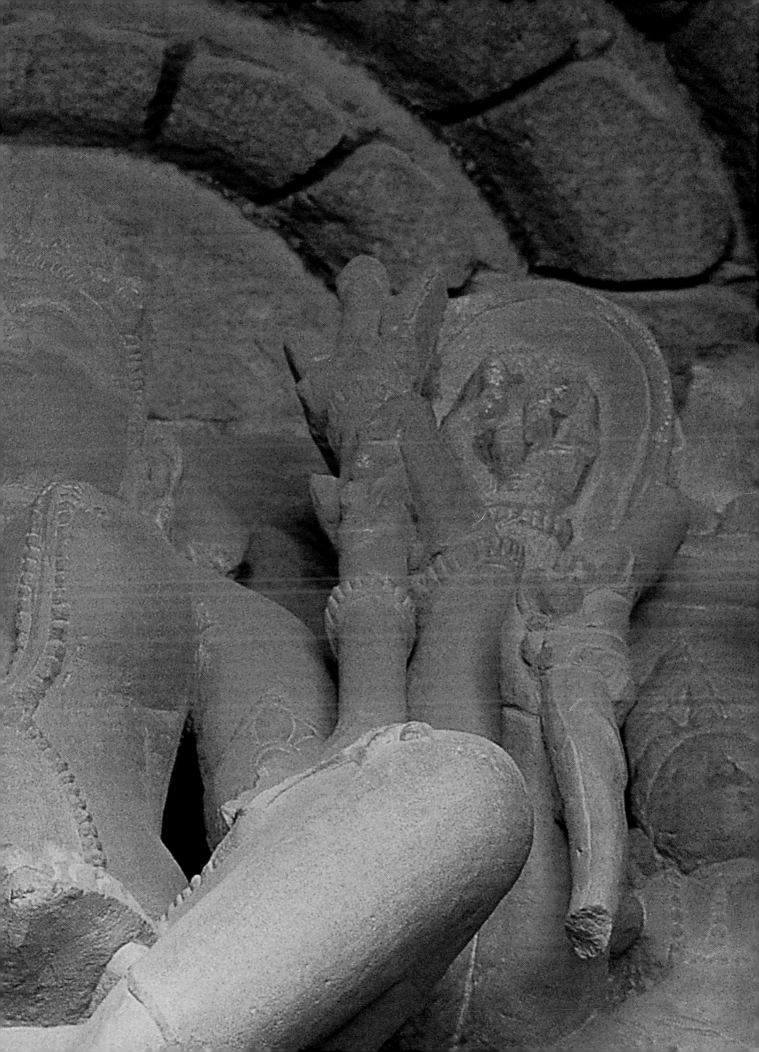

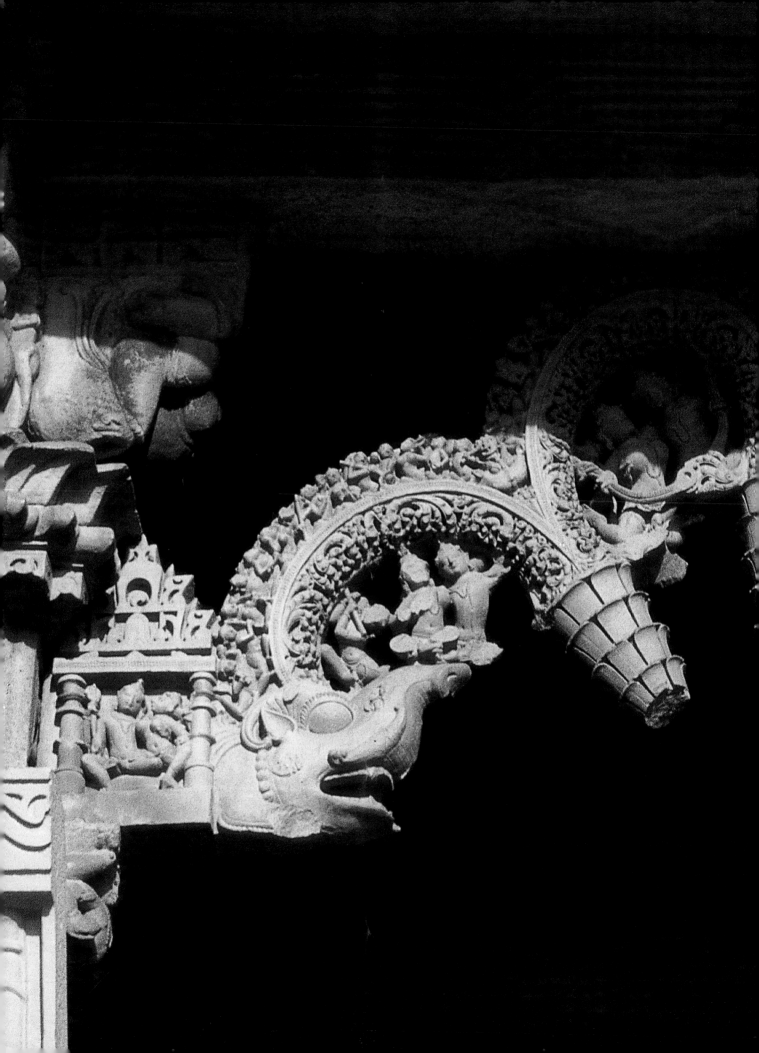

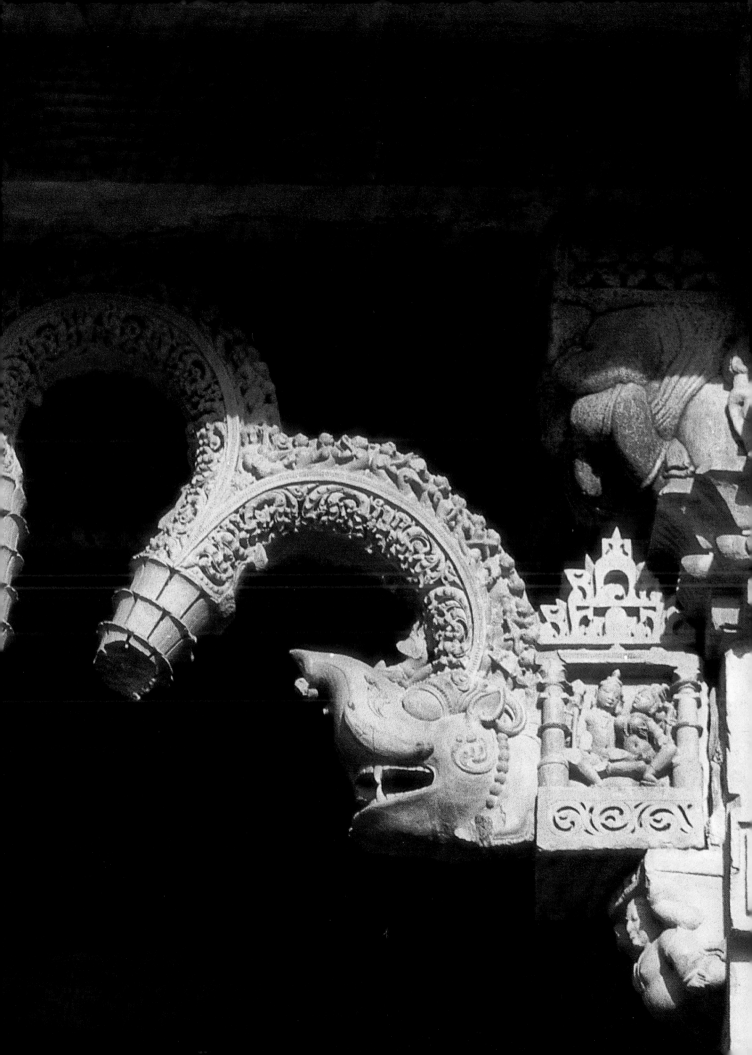

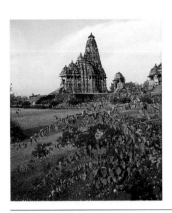

Kandariya Mahadeva

The most perfect specimen of Chandella architecture, the Kandariya Mahadeva temple follows the *panchayatana* plan and has an ambulatory around the sanctum like its predecessors, the Lakshman and Vishvanath temples. The contours of the domical roofs over the *mandapas* rise rhythmically towards the summit of the *shikhara*. Eighty-four *urushringas* cling to the *mulamanjari* creating the magnificent image of mountain peaks. The temple is designed to resemble the sacred cave-residence of Shiva, also known as Mahadeva.

The sculpturing on the *jangha* of the Kandariya Mahadeva is the most elegant at Khajuraho as it marks the culmination of consummate workmanship. There are 646 images on the outer walls, each a model of perfection and rare sophistication. The four-looped *makara-torana* is the most ornamental and exquisitely detailed among Khajuraho's temples. The graded floors of the *mandapas* in the interior lead to the Shiva*Linga* in the sanctum. The ceilings are grand and the sculptured figures on pillars remarkable for their plastic quality. The ambulatory contains some sculptures of the rarest splendour. There are 226 images within the temple's interior.

Art-historian E.B. Havell has great admiration for the remarkable skill which helped the Khajuraho architect achieve a commendable symbiosis of the various structural elements and "with what magnificent imaginative power and technical skill pinnacle upon pinnacle crowned with Vishnu's lotus emblem are piled round the central tower of the shrine to give the impression of the holy mountain upholding the highest heavens. The sculpture in itself is not of the finest art, but nothing could surpass the skill with which details of bewildering complexity are coordinated together in masses so as to form a perfectly balanced architectural unity".

(right): An image of the dancing Ganesh from the Kandariya Mahadev temple. (above): The Kandariya Mahadeva temple is the largest and tallest in Khajuraho, and contains all the elements typical of the architecture that evolved here. It also has the most evolved shikhar. (facing page): Celestial beauties adorning the ceiling of the main hall of the Kandariya Mahadev temple. (preceding page): The makar torana or crocodile-headed arch at the entrance of the Kandariya Mahadeva temple consists of four loops. The brackets and loops in turn are sculptured with images of celestial beings.

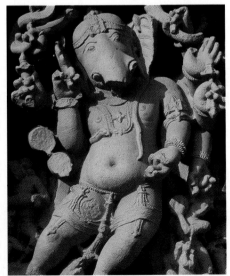

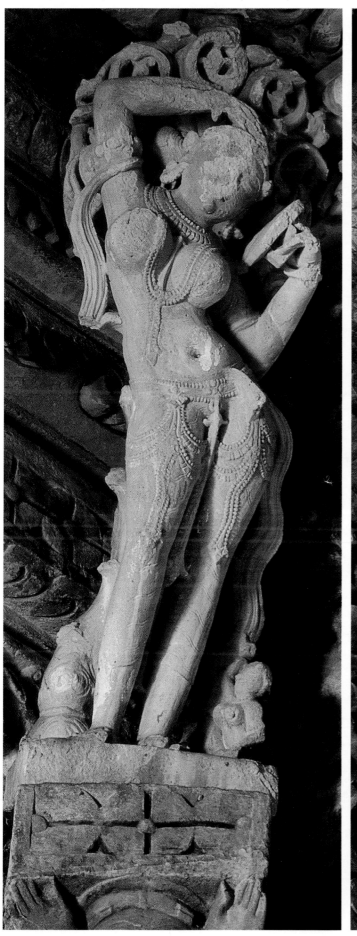
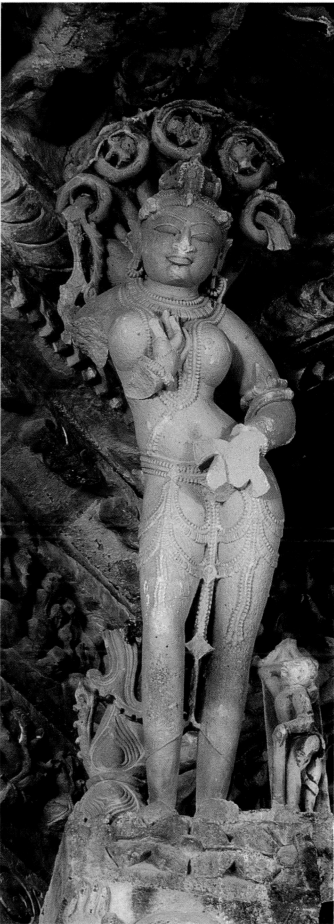

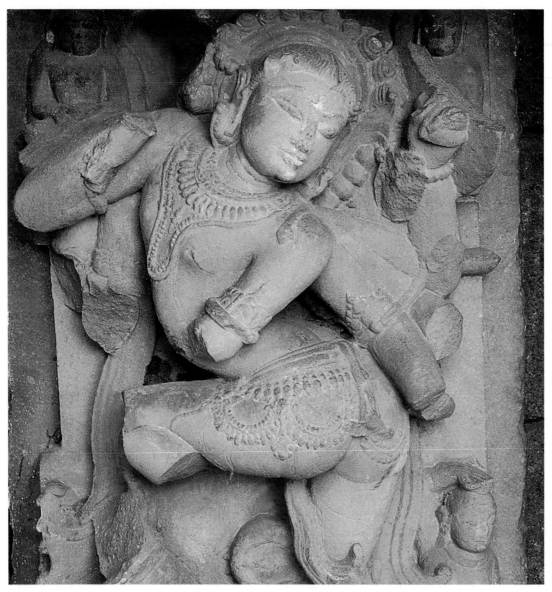

Shantinath

The temple of Shantinath has some ancient sculptures though it has been extensively modernised. The sanctum has a Jain image of Adinath and the temple's oblong enclosure of shrine cells has survived.

Vamana

This temple is dedicated to Vishnu in his incarnation as a dwarf. Modest in size, and without an ambulatory, its porch had collapsed so completely that the restored front has a curious truncated look. With the familiar double band of sculpture on the *jangha*, the Vamana introduces a new feature in the form of female struts in the ceilings of the balconied windows. The sanctum contains a four-armed Vishnu image. The sculpture is impressive.

Javari

This Vishnu temple belongs to the period when Chandella power was on the decline. The sculptured bands on the *jangha* carry some well-proportioned but uninspired statuary, and the number of *urushringas* around the *shikhara* are few. However, its four-looped *makara-torana* decorated with pine cones, lotus scrolls and the flying *gandharvas* is a spectacular piece of sculpture. Standing amidst fields on a high platform, the Javari merits a visit.

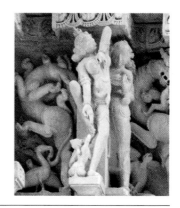

Adinath

Standing adjacent to the Parsvanath, this small temple suffered badly both at the hands of natural forces and the subsequent, incongruous repairs. Still, the *shikhara*, a single spire covered with *chaitya* window motifs, is attractive and the double rows of sculpture contain some excellent pieces. The image of Adinath in the sanctum is modern.

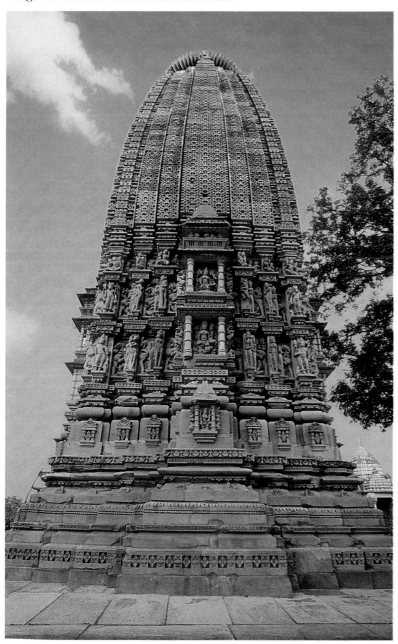

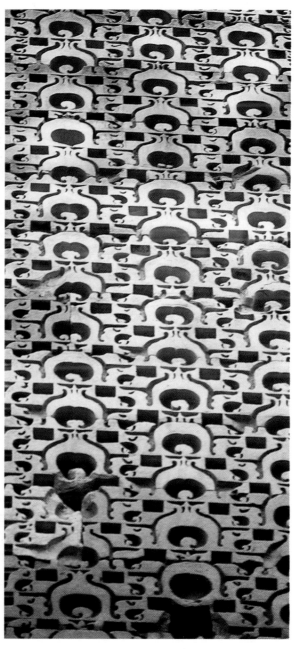

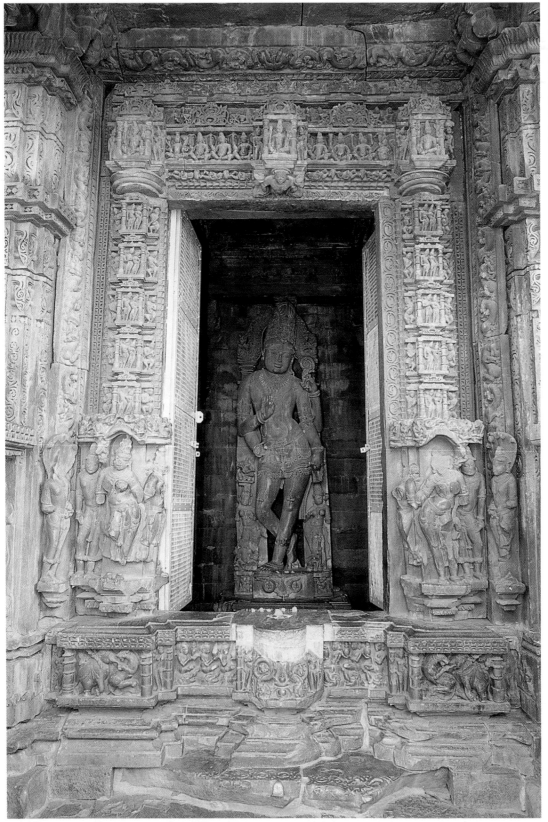

(left): A tall image of a Shiva Dakshinamurti is housed within the sanctum of the Chaturbhuj temple, part of the Southern Group.
(facing page): The Chaturbhuj temple stands on a high platform and, in the absence of spires or turrets, the shikhar has a simple, curvilinear shape.

Chaturbhuj

Two miles south of Khajuraho village, amidst natural wilderness, the Chaturbhuj is the last of the Chandella temples. Considerable restoration of the structure and some still-to-be-finished pieces of sculpture have affected this temple adversely. But the sanctum contains the most exquisite cult image of a 9 ft high Shiva Dakshina*Murti*, a masterpiece of Khajuraho art.

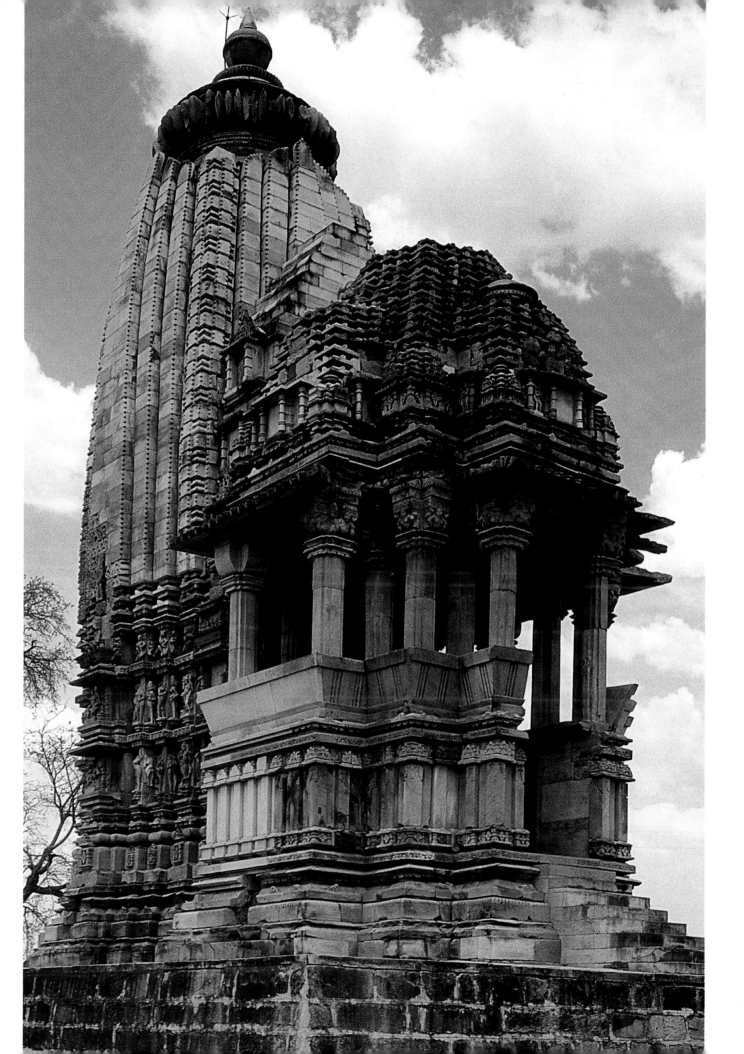

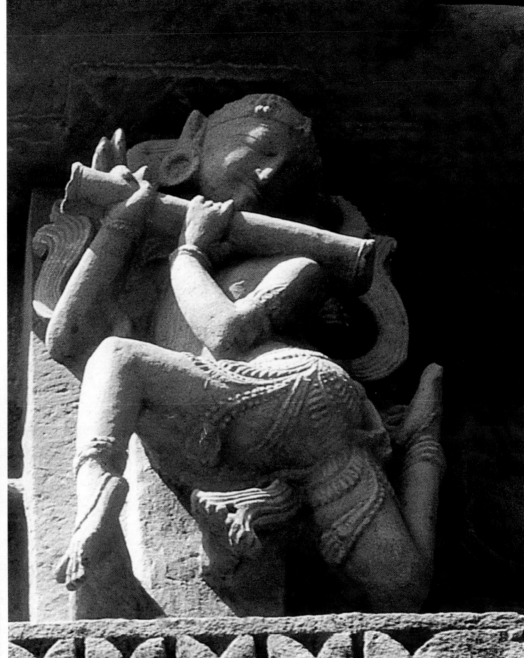

(right): A celestial being with a flute depicts the fluidity of movement captured by the sculptor.
(below): The Duladeo temple, Southern Group, has a tall shikhar surrounded by three rows of minor shikhars and an unusually long entrance chamber.

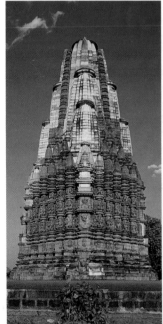

Duladeo

This temple, on the outskirts of the village, belongs to the 12th century when Chandella power was at its lowest ebb. The *shikhara* had almost collapsed but has since been rebuilt in a valiant effort to restore its original grandeur. The Duladeo has the usual components but no ambulatory passage around the sanctum. Sculpture on the *jangha* depicts charming *gandharvas* carrying flowers, playing flutes or brandishing weapons. The *Shalbhanjikas* or tree goddesses on the pillars in the interior have crowns on their head — a new feature.

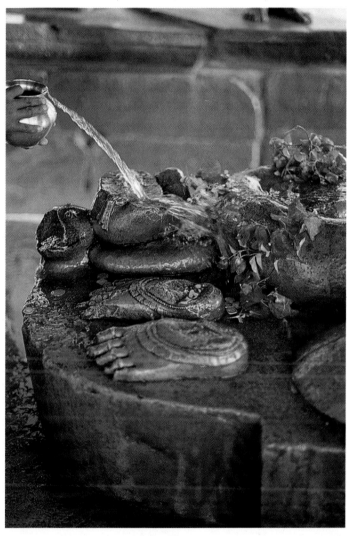

(left): Flowers offered at the entrance of Matangeshwara temple.
(following page):The perfect melding of sculpture and architecture in Khajuraho is best represented by this figure from the Lakshmana temple, which highlights the art that went into its planning, but hides many of the reasons for which these temples were erected.

In addition, there are two more temples in Khajuraho of which note must be made. Sandwiched between the Kandariya Mahadeva and the Devi Jagdamba temples is a small Mahadeva shrine with a magnificently sculptured door and a sculpture of a *sardula* with a human figure kneeling before it, the leit motif of Khajuraho itself, derived from the legend of Chandravarman who founded the Chandella dynasty.

The Western group of temples also contains a small shrine to Devi with a large image of Hanuman near the entrance.

Other than these, Khajuraho Museum is a treasure house of sculptures that have been retrieved from the temples here — those extant as well as others long razed to the ground. Some of the finest masterpieces of Khajuraho sculpture can be seen here.

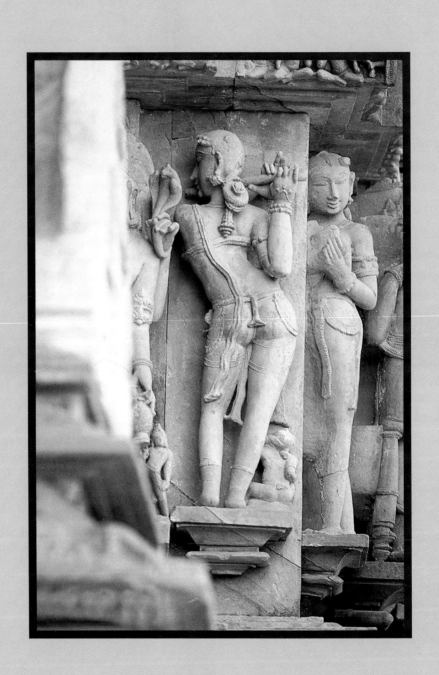